THE
PURPOSE
DIRECTED
BUSINESS

An insider's look into the values, strategies,
and 15 profitability keys of small business success.

DR. KEN GIBSON

Founder & CEO of LearningRx, Inc.
"#1 Ranked Child Enrichment Franchise" –*Entrepreneur Magazine*

WITH JEFFERSON SCOTT

The Purpose Directed Business:
An insider's look into the values, strategies, and 15 profitability keys of small business success.

Published By LearningRx™
5085 List Drive, Suite 200
Colorado Springs, Colorado 80919

Publisher's Cataloging-in-Publication
(Provided by Quality Books, Inc.)

> Gibson, Ken, 1944-
> The purpose directed business : an insider's look
> into the values, strategies, and 15 profitability keys
> of small business success / Ken Gibson ; with Jefferson
> Scott.
> p. cm.
> LCCN 2009925805
> ISBN-13: 978-1-61539-069-4
> ISBN-10: 1-61539-069-3
>
> 1. Small business--Management. 2. Success in
> business. I. Scott, Jefferson. II. Title.

HD62.7.G53 2009   658.02'2
                         QBI09-600051

Library of Congress Control Number: 2009925805

Printed in the United States of America
2009—First Edition

10 9 8 7 6 5 4 3 2

I dedicate this book to my family.

My wife, Sharon, and our five children, Kim, Candy, Tanya, Shawn, Brett, and son-in-laws Wayne, Dean, and Steve.

It has been a privilege watching you grow and an honor sharing my life with you. In this modern era, when families are distant, disjointed and disinterested, you have been different. You are my team, my teachers, my best place on earth. We work each day side by side, and at the end of the day we look forward to the next. I could not have learned God's lessons without you. I am truly blessed and I thank you with all my heart.

—DAD

A happy family is but an earlier heaven.
—John Bowring

TABLE OF CONTENTS

INTRODUCTION

I was almost there.

I was 33 and I already lived in my dream home, the one I'd dreamed of owning when I'd explored the city on my bike as a kid. It had been built in 1907. It was all-brick, had a Spanish tile roof, leaded glass windows, cherry wood-beamed ceilings, and servants' quarters on the third floor.

I owned the most beautiful car ever made: a Jaguar XKE 2+2. Bright yellow. I was a pediatric optometrist with a booming practice. I owned a chain of successful preschools throughout Wisconsin, and held an elected political office. I owned more than 30 apartment buildings and was raking in gross revenues of almost $150,000 per month (in today's dollars). I had it all: growing assets, a beautiful wife, the first three of my five children, and success wherever I turned. I was well on the way to reaching my goal of becoming a millionaire by the time I turned 35.

But I was miserable.

Life had no meaning to me. If I'd ever had a real purpose, I'd lost it. My life was way too complex. Morally, I was spiraling downward. My choice of friends had changed for the worse. My marriage was deteriorating.

I was living for myself—because in our culture, that's the way you live if you can afford to, right? Although I had discovered that the financial pursuit did not satisfy me as I'd always thought it would, I didn't know what else to do. I was sinking into despair, though on the outside, I was the picture of success.

I thought maybe the solution would be to shift from trying to build wealth to trying to build personal comfort. If I could just control the people around me so they did what I wanted, I would be happy. It's the logical conclusion of a self-centered person, which I certainly was. So that was what I did for the next 20 years of my life.

It wasn't until I was in my late 50s and should've known better that I finally got a clue. My 80-year-old Aunt Mary from Phoenix came to visit my mother, who lived in the garden level of our home. During the course of visiting with Aunt Mary I happened to pick up a book she was reading. I opened it and read the first sentence.

"It's not about you."

That hit me right between the eyes. I couldn't tear my eyes from the page. *It's not about me? Of course it is. Who else is there?* The next paragraph drove the knife in deeper:

> The purpose of your life is far greater than your own personal fulfillment, your peace of mind, or even your happiness. It's far greater than your family, your career, or even your wildest dreams and ambitions. If you want to know why you were placed on this planet, you must begin with God. You were born by His purpose and for His purpose.

These are the opening lines from a little book called *The Purpose Driven Life* by Rick Warren.

In that moment my life was forever changed. I took Aunt Mary's book and found a corner of my house to sit down and read. You're supposed to go through *The Purpose Driven Life* over the course of 40 days but I read it all in one sitting. That's saying a lot for a guy with dyslexia. I inhaled it. Absorbed it. I let it permeate me and sink in down deep. Sometimes I had to stop reading because I was bawling so hard.

At the end of that reading I was left with one shining truth dominating my mind: My life was all wrong. Everything I'd done I'd done to please myself. The things and people around me were trophies, testimonials to my ability to twist the world to my benefit. I was the high priest of the Church of Dr. Kenneth Herbert Gibson.

But it was all ash.

Suddenly God had my attention. I'd been a Christian virtually all my life but obviously had gotten the First Commandment wrong. It's hard to worship at the First Church of Gibson and yet have no other gods before the real God.

The next day I went to Sam's Club and purchased 100 copies of *The Purpose Driven Life*. I began giving them away like tickets to the last lifeboat on the *Titanic*. I gave one to the person in line behind me, another to the cashier, and another to someone in the parking lot. I knew firsthand the liberation God was bringing through this book and I wanted everyone around me to feel as free as I did.

For the first time in my life, it really wasn't all about me.

On that day God began renovating my life. Since then I've been down roads I never would've considered taking when I was the one driving the bus. I saw what it meant to be a servant leader—a concept I would never have come to on my own.

Suddenly my life was imbued with purpose. I now had marching orders for tasks that would expand His kingdom, not mine. I understood the wisdom and benefits of value-centered business. And I'm still being worked on.

Which brings us to you.

Welcome to the Family

I have written this book especially for you, the new LearningRx franchisee, as well as others who want the inside scoop of how to really succeed in a small business.

(A note to non-franchisees: There is a reason why franchised businesses are eight times more likely to succeed than independent businesses – and it's not that they make a better hamburger. There is a system, a proven way of doing things. There is support, help to guide you to better decisions. There is savings, due to shared marketing development and system volume. And there is the franchisor evaluating your skills and requiring that you have enough capital. This book contains many "good business practices" and a few seldom-shared "great business secrets" that will help any business owner. I know that you will benefit from reading these values, strategies, and key profitability ideas.)

You've come to invest in LearningRx because you've seen what the program can do and you want to be part of changing lives.

You believe in it, and for that I thank you. I welcome you into the LearningRx family with open arms. I'm personally pulling for your success.

In order to give you the best chance of achieving that success, I'm going to ask you to allow me to share with you what I have learned about business. Many of these lessons came after that critical day in the early 2000s, but many of them were good practices I had learned before that. Just remember that these practices work as they should only when you too realize that it's not all about you.

This book is laid out in three major sections: Values, Strategies, and Profitability. In the section on values I talk about foundational issues like purpose, integrity, taking responsibility, and excellence. In the section on strategies I talk about business issues like vision, building a team, and serving. In the profitability section I share 15 keys to profitability and the resulting use of those profits in the chapter on stewardship and sharing.

In these pages I have attempted to download myself, my entire business sense, into a form you can take and apply in your own life and work. You already have excellent instincts and experience of your own. These will enhance the knowledge in this book, creating the optimum composite for success.

LearningRx works. The procedures are astonishingly effective. But the business model *behind* the system works, too. That's important because, even if you have the best product in the world, if your business model is flawed you'll have endless struggles—and the world may never then get the chance to see how great your product is.

Read the lessons in this book. Apply them to your life (hopefully in a less painful fashion than what I had to go through to learn them). Adopt this thinking into your business leadership. When you do, your LearningRx franchise, not to mention your personal life, will be positioned for success. Success as God defines it.

Today I don't have the passion for material wealth I had back when I was 33. I live in a different house and I no longer drive a Jag. But I restored the relationship with my wife, that had been suffering; I emerged from my moral slide. I made the right kind of friends. And I found my purpose.

So read on. Learn how to run your LearningRx franchise as I now run the entire LearningRx corporation. And between the lines of the pages of this book, you may just find your purpose as well.

SECTION 1

Values

CHAPTER 1

Find Purpose

THE NOVEL *STORM WARRIORS* by Jon Nappa begins with a gripping scene of calamity at sea. The real-life story is set in 19th-century England in the age of sailing ships. As the book begins, the captain of a schooner is skirting the coast of Britain at night during a fierce storm. Though it is pitch-black, he knows the area well and seeks out the landmarks he expects.

Suddenly he spots lights. He thinks at first they must be lights marking the land, so he orients the ship accordingly. But the lights begin to sway, leading the captain and his crew to believe they must've gotten turned around in the night and what they're really seeing are lights from another ship being tossed about by the storm.

This changes his whole perspective. What he thought was land is really open sea, which meant he must reverse direction or smash into the reef.

He turns the ship around despite the wrath of the sea, but is astonished to sight waves crashing on the rocks directly before him. He has no time to turn. The wind and surf drive him directly onto the reef. The ship is destroyed and everyone but one on board is lost.

We learn later that the lights were indeed from the land. They were the work of a local resident hoping to confuse passing ships and cause them to wreck—so that he could lay claim to the bounty that would wash ashore afterward.

Deceptive Guides

Ever feel like this doomed captain? Ever feel like you're trying to get somewhere good but the directions you're following are driving you to shipwreck instead?

Perhaps you're going along in life and someone tells you that you ought to be going in a certain direction, so you change course. Maybe your own sense of direction causes you to suspect you're not heading the right way so you make another course correction, only to be redirected again the next day. In the end, you find that not only did you not get where you wanted but you're in dire straits: taking on water and being smashed by the storm.

This is what comes of following deceptive guides.

That's what I was like. For the first 50 years of my life I thought I knew where I wanted to go and how to get there, but in reality I was adrift. Lost at sea. I would achieve a goal but still wouldn't feel I had arrived. I would feel empty. So I would head out in a new direction, chasing a new goal, only to find that the next one left me empty as well.

Someone charting my course over those years would've seen me zigging and zagging across the map, doubling back, getting lost—and coming dangerously close to a few reefs.

I was following deceptive guides. I thought I knew my destination, but really I didn't. I was led around by false lights and a few areas of my life almost ended in shipwreck, destroyed on the rocks.

A Constant Light

What we're talking about here is purpose. A person without a purpose is like a ship tossed about on the waves, heading this way and that and ultimately ending in destruction.

People and causes on all sides will say they are the right direction for you to follow. Our society itself espouses a number of paths it says are worthy of your time and money. It's hard to know whether you should support Greenpeace or the Salvation Army, whether you should vote pro-life or pro-immigration or pro-drilling, or whether you should buy Girl Scout cookies or avoid saturated fats. You could go crazy trying to please everyone and trying to follow every light you see out in a storm.

What you need is a *purpose*, an understanding of what you're here to do. A guiding purpose will unify your thoughts and make sense of all the competing voices calling to you. A strong purpose will help you know which opportunities to avail yourself of and which ones it's OK to say no to. A purpose, like the constant light from a lighthouse, will take you surely to the port you were heading toward.

What is your purpose? Do you have one that towers over

the others? Is it a healthy purpose? You've got to have that one guiding light. Perhaps becoming part of the LearningRx family has to do with your purpose.

Purpose Gives Meaning to Your Life

You have chosen to become part of the LearningRx family. Why?

I've heard as many reasons as there are franchisees. Some say they did it because it was a good fit for their past experiences. Some like the idea of being their own boss. Some list the income potential or a love of children as their reasons. Some like that LearningRx is something they can do as a family.

But the one comment I've heard from almost everyone is this: "I want to do something that gives meaning to my life." Yes, we all want to live a life of meaning.

I believe our Creator considers people to be His ultimate purpose. If that is the case, then people ought to be *our* purpose, too. It should be people—not the accumulation of things or the attempt to please everyone or the desire to become famous—that are the constant light guiding our voyage.

A purpose instills your life with a sense of meaning.

Purpose Produces Passion

A purpose will motivate your life. It will get you up in the morning and keep you going when others stop. A purpose will fill your days with passion.

I have a friend named Ro (Rochunga Pudaite), who grew up

in northeast India. His grandfather was a headhunter who was given a little book, the Gospel of John, in their tribal language, and as a result the whole tribe converted to Christianity.

Later, at the age of 10, Ro became determined to translate the whole Bible into his tribal language. He walked 96 miles through tiger-infested jungles to get to the mission school that would start him on his journey. There he learned to read and write. Eventually Ro came to America to attend Wheaton College, where he completed translating the entire Bible into his tribal language.

The one comment I've heard from almost everyone is this: "I want to do something that gives meaning to my life."

Ro's purpose fueled his passion. And now that passion has extended beyond a translation. Ro's ministry has sent more than 16 million Bibles into more than 100 countries.

I have another friend whose purpose has impacted me greatly. I first met Gerard and his family as my patients when Gerard was in sixth grade. He was slow in speech, couldn't ride a bike or dribble a basketball, and was having difficulty in school. He wanted to be a good farmer like his dad. He wanted his parents to be proud of him. He loved his farm.

We put Gerard into the brain training program that eventually became LearningRx. Though he had many handicaps, he was one of the most determined patients I've ever had. He knew that to be a good farmer he would need good eye-hand coordination around equipment. Within a few months, his motor integration skills improved to the point that he was dribbling a basketball while riding his bike. His hard work and passion were rewarded 12 years later, when he was named Outstanding Young Farmer of the Year.

What have you been given? What opportunities have been handed to you? More than others? Fewer? It doesn't matter. What matters is how faithfully you deal with what you have been given, how faithfully you use your opportunities to fulfill your purpose.

There's a story about three servants of a rich man. The rich man had to journey to another country but he left money with his servants and instructed them to invest it until his return. One servant ended up making a tenfold profit on what he'd been given, and was rewarded greatly upon his master's return. Another made a fivefold return. The third simply buried his money and gave it back to the master. The master cursed this servant for not doing anything useful with what he'd been given.

So it is with purpose. We've been given a certain amount of resources and opportunities, and we're expected to invest them wisely. We can invest what has been given us or we can refuse to do anything with what we are given. What are you doing with what you've been given?

Purpose Simplifies Your Life

One of the chief benefits of having a strong purpose guiding you is that it brings focus to your life. When you understand what you're supposed to be doing you instantly know what things must be done and what things can safely be skipped. Suddenly, you don't feel bad saying no to the various causes that come your way, because you know what you're about and where you can do the most good.

John Gillespie was my closest adult friend in my late teens. He arranged the circumstances that brought my wife, Sharon, and me together. In his late 20s he was determined to help troubled teenage boys, so he founded Rawhide Boys Ranch, which has since become the model for many other boys' homes.

John's purpose was so focused that nothing could stop him. Though he was an unknown person, he was able to recruit Bart Starr, the legendary Green Bay Packers quarterback, as an active spokesman. John got a local TV station to run a telethon for years. He even became the major recipient of donated cars in the state of Wisconsin. That very same purpose-directed passion has never wavered. Recently, again as an unknown, John ran a close U.S. Senate race against the very popular Herb Kohl.

John illustrates how purpose will provide you with focus. But not everyone's focus becomes as outwardly known as John's. And that's fine, because our gifts and talents don't determine our success.

My wife's mom was a very private person whose passion was not diminished even with big changes in her life. She became blind right before I met my wife. When she lost her sight, she devoted herself to prayer. She became the most dedicated, persistent intercessory prayer warrior I have ever known. When she died, I felt a great loss—not simply because she was gone, but because I no longer had someone so devoted to petitioning God on my behalf.

Purpose brings clarity to the large and small decisions of

your life. It brings decisiveness. I have come to understand that decisiveness is not so much the ability to think quickly as the ability to compare the opportunity with your purpose. If some opportunity comes along that is good but doesn't match up with your purpose, you can discard it—and people will think you're just a marvelous decision-maker!

Purpose trumps profit. A meaningful life's work is better than any job description.

Recently, I made several trips to visit most of our LearningRx centers. I was traveling with family across the country and I needed to be in good spirits when I arrived at each center. But I also needed to have energy and to enjoy time with my family. Therefore, I couldn't drain myself by having to be CEO all day. I decided to limit myself to four hours of being CEO/Visiting Dignitary every day. Knowing my purpose allowed me to see clearly what needed to be done.

What's your purpose? When you know it, it will focus and simplify your life. Many major decisions will become easy. Knowing your purpose will give you passion. It will help you make the most of the opportunities given you. It will give your life meaning. And it will act like a lighthouse guiding your way through a dark and treacherous sea.

Before I found my own guiding purpose I just…existed. I plodded through each day – surviving. I did all the things I was supposed to do. I made money to pay bills. But I lacked purpose. It was an empty existence.

When I did find a meaning for my life after the age of 50,

everything changed. Now, my life flows out of my purpose. Now my purpose directs and informs everything I do. It affects where I spend my money, how I spend my time, and how I handle every conversation. I filter my decisions with, "Why am I here right now? Why are we having this discussion? How does this tie back to my purpose?"

This new focus frees me up. I can easily move from one thing to another—even changing directions in what I'm doing—so long as I'm always moving toward that purpose. I feel comfortable where I am right now, but if a new way opened up that more perfectly pointed me toward my purpose, I would be able to make that change just fine.

Someone without a purpose wanders around in the dark, not knowing over what he stumbles, not knowing where he's even trying to get. Someone with a purpose may still be in the dark and may still occasionally stumble over hidden obstacles, but he'll never wonder where he's going. He may have to skirt around this or turn to avoid that, but always he is moving toward that constant light.

Purpose at Work

Your purpose should allow you to live your values and beliefs in all parts of your life, including the workplace.

As you think about your employees, you need to help them see the purpose and meaning in what they do, too. They need to understand that they're part of something wonderful. You can help them see this by getting to know their desires and passions— and helping them achieve them.

Sometimes that means encouraging them to follow their purpose even if they have to leave your employment to do so. It's hard to lose a valuable staff member—but people are more important than things—and therefore helping others fulfill their passion and purpose is of greater value than our convenience. Besides, we now gain the opportunity to contribute to a new staff member's life.

Working to live out your purpose is far superior to working to make a living.

If you are working just to earn a paycheck, then your attitude toward others—even clients and those working for you—will be to use and manipulate rather than to serve. If you use some people, like your employees, and serve others, like your family, then you are compartmentalizing the secular and spiritual parts of your life. You're saying that some people are of value and others are not.

Purpose trumps profit. A meaningful life's work is better than any job description. Your purpose, when you find it, can and must be lived out in the workplace. To not do so is to make your heart sick.

What you believe about your purpose will determine your values. And your values will affect how you behave.

Conclusion

As you can see, this book will not be your average get-rich-quick instruction manual. You are important and of great value. Your purpose matters, not only to you but to me. Many success authors would teach you just to work hard or to manipulate people to get ahead. But I would rather face the judgment of other business leaders than to direct your thinking down the wide path that leads to personal failure. I am committed to helping you find your purpose.

It is unfortunate that it took me so long to learn this lesson. I'd had the concept of a guiding purpose presented to me all my life—I just had a different agenda and wasn't listening. As a result, and after much heartache, after many years I have established in my heart what should have been there from the beginning.

My life has found purpose near its end, but in this book I've put purpose at the beginning in Chapter 1—for your sake.

There are many deceitful lights surrounding you in the night, many false guides that would lead you to shipwreck. But when you find your true purpose, your constant light, you can trust it to lead you safely home.

CHAPTER 2

Live with Integrity

I STOOD BEFORE A ROOM full of doctors. It was one of my first cognitive training seminars with psychologists and I, an eye doctor, was introducing the cognitive concepts that eventually came to be known as LearningRx.

The talk was going well. It's no small thing to see scores of professionals feverishly taking notes over something you're teaching them. I admit my ego was feeling pretty inflated. I made a joke to the group and checked out the response with my daughter and son-in-law, who were at the back of the room. They looked a little uneasy, but I dismissed it and went on.

I concluded that section, answered a few questions, and called a 10-minute break. At the rear of the room I noticed my daughter and son-in-law. They still looked a little uncomfortable, so I worked my way back to them. They asked to have a private word with me, so we excused ourselves and found a quiet spot.

"Dad," my daughter Tanya said, "Dean and I are uncomfortable with some of the things you said just now."

"And not just that last section," Dean said, "but in a number of your presentations here so far."

What was this? Mutiny in the ranks? The seminar had been a huge success so far. What could I have possibly said wrong? "All right," I said as graciously as I could manage, "tell me what you mean."

Tanya and Dean proceeded to describe what they saw as a number of…exaggerations…from my talks. I had claimed that we were working with 300 or so doctors and had helped more than 10,000 patients, when in fact the numbers were lower, about 285 doctors and 8,000 students. Tanya reminded me of a line from a song she had learned years before: "Stretching the truth is telling a lie."

I had to admit it: They had me.

A bunch of excuses jumped into my mind. I'd grown up stretching the truth to stay out of trouble or to make myself look better, so really it was the fault of my upbringing that I stretched the truth now and then. Plus, I had an Irish heritage—blame it on the Blarney Stone! It was strange: When I used to hear my father exaggerate it would really bother me, and now here I was caught following in his footsteps.

But it was my Christian scruples, more than the challenge from my loved ones, that brought conviction on this matter. I was misleading people in order to advance myself. That was wrong no matter how I looked at it.

What was I to do? Could I stand before those doctors and

admit I'd been fibbing? I could just imagine the hit my credibility was going to take. Could this cognitive training material—about which there was no lie—be considered legitimate if its originator was proved a liar?

In short, my integrity was on the line. And not just my integrity but the integrity of all I had worked to achieve. Shoot, I was even in danger of damaging the integrity of my daughter and the rest of my family.

Something had to change.

At that moment I decided I would confess my errors. I went back into the room and corrected my exaggerations and authorized my family to confront me at every break in any seminars during which they felt I had not been truthful. I agreed that if I made the slightest exaggeration in my talk I would, after the break, confess to the group my untruths and correct my misstatements.

With that kind of consequence hanging over me, you can imagine how long it took me to change my ways. Not long at all!

That policy holds to this day. Happily, it seems to have broken me of my exaggerations. I can't remember the last time I had to go back and correct a misstatement. Indeed, these days I'm more likely to understate than overstate. And that's the truth.

How's Your Integrity?

Your truthfulness is the largest factor in establishing trust in the minds of people around you. Your staff, customers, and vendors need to know that you are a person of your word and that your word is not an exaggeration.

Indeed, there is no attribute more important to success in a business relationship than integrity. Integrity is the quality that guarantees the other attributes. You need to be the type of person whose personal values and morals are beyond question.

Integrity is at the heart of character. You've heard the old adage that character is who you are when no one is looking. You must maintain integrity and truthfulness in all your dealings. In business, as in life, everything counts.

A Matter of Trust

When I was challenged to stop stretching the truth, I was really being asked to become a person worthy of trust.

You must gain the trust of those working with you. Trust is the foundation of real teamwork. Indeed, trust gives freedom, just as telling the truth brings freedom—because you no longer have to remember all the lies you told to each person. Behave honestly, live in a trustworthy manner, and you'll make life much easier for yourself.

How do you build trust? By living in line with the values you profess. If you think stealing is wrong, do you give less value than for what you are paid? If you disapprove of gossiping, do you do it? If you insist your staff members make it to work on time, do you regularly come in late? If you want people telling you the truth, do you tell little white lies?

The part of you that other people see is like the tip of the proverbial iceberg. You are more than what you show the world. So it is with those around you. But if what you attempt to show to the world isn't who you really are, eventually that will come out.

A person who says one thing but lives another way is a hypocrite, unworthy of trust.

The benefit of behaving uprightly is that, when your heart and head are clear of deception, your actions are aligned with your values. You become a person of integrity.

A Trusting Team

Truthfulness establishes trust with others.

When you have trust among your team members, you have a real team. A group of people who do not trust each other is not a team at all.

Building trust among your staff is a vital task for you as a LearningRx franchisee. It starts with you living consistently with your own stated values and by you holding yourself to a high standard of integrity. But trust extends to your employees as well.

Your staff members need to know your intentions are good, so they have no reason to hold back true honesty. They need to know they can open up to you and to each other without fear of betrayal. They need to feel they can admit their mistakes and fears and weaknesses without worrying about reprisals.

When your team members see you living with integrity they will be inspired to do so as well. And a LearningRx center characterized by integrity will be a LearningRx center people recommend.

Building Character

Ralph Waldo Emerson said, "No change of circumstances can repair a defect of character."

Over time, your behavior will display how you have prioritized your values. This hierarchy of values is revealed with or without your permission. Ultimately, you will live out your values, whatever they are.

How do you develop character? Embrace pain. Learn from it. Don't waste your suffering: Let it be an opportunity for growth. There is never a straight path to success. It is a maze filled with obstacles. Don't let the obstacles stop you. Keep moving forward. A clear understanding of your purpose will help you to go around, jump over, or break through your obstacles. Life is a test. Character is developed and revealed through it. Nothing is insignificant.

Here's a story from my daughter Candy:

After spending a couple of weeks in second grade I went to my dad with a complaint about my teacher. I thought she really disliked me and was way too strict. Since my dad was the administrator at the school I thought for sure he could do something to improve my classroom situation.

I remember sharing with him for quite a while all the horrible things this teacher was doing. I really thought by the end of the conversation that my dad was going to save me from my horrible circumstance. Then to my dismay, he told me, "Great, Candy—you get to grow some character." I left the room wondering what that meant, and disappointed that I did not get my way.

This was the answer that my dad continuously presented to me throughout my life whenever I found myself in a difficult situation. As the years went on I began to understand what that meant and I am now able to embrace hardships, knowing that they will help me grow character.

Principles vs. Profits

As a business owner you will be tempted to choose expediency over integrity, to do the thing you believe is needed rather than the thing you believe is right. But I can tell you that principles and profits are not opposites— you can do what's right and still be successful.

Also, it's never too late to do the right thing. Recently, one of my children handed me $13, confessing that this amount had been taken off my dresser more than 10 years before. Imagine the sense of freedom and removal of guilt experienced after righting a wrong.

Profit and growth result from the pursuit of your purpose. Now we have a built-in desire to add to and connect with others in a significant way.

Conclusion

Hopefully, you will never find yourself called to account for blatant untruths you have told to a room full of doctors. Hopefully, you will not have people questioning your integrity as a businessperson. Hopefully, your staff will not have to work for a boss who demands one thing of his employees but applies a more lenient set of rules to himself.

However, if you know you do have issues of integrity that need to be cleared up—and most of us do—I hope you have someone who will confront you about them. Someone like my daughter and son-in-law. Indeed, this very chapter ought to challenge you to be sure your life is lived out in consistency with what you say you believe.

Integrity, marked by truthfulness and trustworthiness, is a hallmark of LearningRx in general. And it must be at the heart of your center as well.

Every man, at the bottom of his heart, wants to do right. But only he can do right who knows right; only he knows right who thinks right; only he thinks right who believes right. —TIORIO

CHAPTER 3

Take Responsibility

I'LL START THIS CHAPTER with a story from my oldest daughter, Kim:

> *"Take responsibility" seemed like my dad's favorite phrase as I was growing up. My sisters and I were required to buy our own clothes starting at age 10. To earn money, Dad would often hire us to work in one of his businesses. He always started out by telling us that we had to "own the job"—then he would tell us what was to be achieved and we had to figure out how to do it. He wouldn't tell us what to do—we had to ask and find out from him and others. He made us responsible not only for doing our job but also for learning it. Here's an example:*
>
> *While I was in fourth grade, my dad asked me if I would be interested in having my own line of greeting*

cards. Make my own cards? That would be awesome!
I could be like a real artist.

So I went about drawing until my dad said it was
perfect. One card had a cow with large udders and said,
"Wisconsin, the udder most part of the world." Another
said, "Love Is Sharing" and showed two dogs sharing one
bone. Another said, "You're Special" with a frog on a
mushroom.

Dad asked me, "If someone got your card and wanted
to buy more of them, how would they know about you and
how could you make your cards extra special?"

I finally came up with the idea of writing on the back
of each card. "Hi, my name is Kimmy Gibson, age 9, and
I think you're special because God made you. If you would
like more of my cards write to me at 312 N. Union Street,
Appleton, WI 54911."

We had them printed and I packaged them in plastic
bags. I was very proud of them and took them to show
Dad. "They look great!" he said. "Now go and sell them."

Sell them? I had to sell them? I was only 9, how was
I going to do that?

"Door to door," he said. "You're smart—you'll figure
it out. Go around the neighborhood. You need to sell 10
packages before you come back."

"Do I get to keep the money?" I asked.

"Yes, after you've paid off the expenses of the printing."

At $2 a pack I would have to sell about 40 packages of cards before I made my first dime!

Going door to door was hard. I felt pretty shy about knocking on doors, not knowing who was going to open the door or what to say. But I learned how to talk to adults and how to sell. I learned that old ladies liked package deals, which got me home quicker. For weeks, every day I had to hit the streets and sell my cards.

My dad taught me that you have to do more than dream. You need to plan, figure out the process, and then have the determination and passion to make the dream come true. I wasn't allowed to blame the weather, the competition, or the neighborhood. My success was my responsibility! My cards got around. Twelve years later I was still filling orders—mostly from little old ladies.

A Hero Arises

Taking responsibility is the act of refusing to pass off to someone else an act that must be done. It means looking a requirement in the face and doing your best to meet it. Often, it means taking a harder, lonelier path, a path few others may travel. It means taking on the burden of doing the right thing even if you must stand alone to do so.

Responsibility is an essential quality in business, as in life. There are easier ways to operate than the way of responsibility. Sounding good in the moment but having no intention of fulfilling your promises, for instance. Or shrugging your shoulders and walking away when things get tough. Not standing up for someone when it is in your power to do so. An irresponsible life is the path of the sluggard and the coward.

It requires a certain brand of heroism to take responsibility. Indeed, you could almost define a hero as someone who endeavors to do the right thing even when it's difficult.

When things go well, look through the window; when things go badly, look in the mirror.

As a LearningRx franchisee, you'll have many, many opportunities to be a hero. In the lives of the students your center touches, in their families' lives, and in the lives of your employees, your willingness to take responsibility will serve you well.

You'll show your heroic willingness to take responsibility in four areas: accepting responsibility for your own actions, maintaining a positive attitude, being decisive, and being determined.

Personal Responsibility

I have a saying that those around me hear often: When things go well, look through the window; when things go badly, look in the mirror.

When your LearningRx center is doing very well, use that as an opportunity to praise everyone around you. Look out the window—figuratively speaking— to spot the people on your team upon whom you can lavish accolades and encouragement.

But when struggles come it's no longer the time to look out the window. That's not the moment to hand out blame to your staff. When hard times come, that's your opportunity to look in the mirror, to examine yourself to see what can be done to bring improvement.

Taking responsibility means pointing at yourself for any lack of positive results. It means no excuses. It means pinning on your own chest the onus for why things are in a downturn and accepting the task of turning things around.

Even when things are going well, personal responsibility means fostering in yourself a hunger for improvement. It means you are not sitting back and letting others take the lead when it comes to finding ways to enhance your success, strengthen your team, and raise the satisfaction of your customers.

I learned responsibility early in my own life. My parents' style of parenting allowed me to take charge of myself and my four younger brothers. When I was 12, I started my very first business: a lawn-mowing service with three employees. And when I was 16 I had a painting business with five employees. We painted nine houses our first summer. Through those adventures I learned the benefits of being a responsible worker and having responsible workers.

At one of the houses we were painting, my best friend, Larry, dropped a gallon of white paint from a ladder. The spill covered about 25 square feet of lawn. He assured me that he would take care of it—and he did. The next morning it was replaced by a far nicer lawn. It wasn't until I got a call from his mom that night that I learned he had fulfilled his responsibility by removing 25 square feet of his parents' front lawn!

Eight years later on my 24th birthday, I decided to take personal responsibility for my livelihood. In a northern Wisconsin cabin, in tears, I informed my dad that I could not continue in practice with him, that my nature required me to take control and be responsible for my own future and success.

Taking personal responsibility is the first attribute of the kind of heroic responsibility you'll need to thrive as a LearningRx franchisee.

Maintaining a Positive Attitude

The second attribute you need is a positive outlook. The benefits you'll receive by infecting your center with a happy attitude about your work are many. It will uplift your staff, yourself, and every family who walks through your door.

The opposite is also true. "Stinkin' thinkin'" will harm your center in more ways than you can imagine. Your employees will dread coming to work and your students will fail to achieve to their potential. New families will feel it just walking in to your center. You'll never know the level of success you would've reached had you just maintained a positive attitude about your work. This is one of the intangibles that will permeate every aspect of what happens at your center.

A few years ago I felt like I was in a funeral home each time I entered our own center. After sitting there for awhile trying to figure out why it felt like that, it became apparent that our reliable receptionist liked order, control, and quiet—requiring kids to behave as if they were in a highly disciplined classroom. Within weeks of replacing her, the center was filled with excitement and energy and referrals were up.

You can set the tone—the atmosphere—of wherever you work.

Even though it may not be your nature to do this, raising your energy level will help others enjoy their work and look forward to going to work every day. A dishwasher can create poems and songs for the cooks. The bus driver can greet passengers as they get on and, as they get off, encourage them with a "Have a great day."

What can you do to set the tone in your center? Yes, this takes effort, but the mood it creates will make the day so much more enjoyable.

This works with people as well. At age 4, my second daughter, Candy, was constantly pouting and complaining. Getting her to do anything was a fight. So I gave her a new nickname— Happy Helpful. The change was immediate. She lived up to her nickname, and even today she is the happiest, most helpful person I know.

Life is too short to go around moping. Nurturing negative thinking about someone else is like taking poison and waiting for the other person to die. Add a positive attitude to your acceptance of personal responsibility, and your LearningRx Center will thrive.

Decisiveness

The third component of a LearningRx franchisee who is taking heroic responsibility is decisiveness.

Successful people are decisive people. They don't make hasty decisions just for the sake of looking decisive, however. They gather all the information they need to make an informed decision and then they act without delay. They do not procrastinate.

The Nike® tagline "Just do it"™ would benefit many. Too many think so long over decisions that they end up never making any. I believe this is because many people aren't sure where they are going. They don't know their purpose. Therefore, they don't know how to compare the options before them and decide which one is best.

As I think back over my life and review the major decisions I've made, I can see how much less full my life would have been and how many opportunities I would have missed if I had not made those decisions. I'll share one as an example.

After graduation from college I returned to my home community of Appleton, Wisconsin. Some friends asked me to join them in the study of a new book: How to Turn $1,000 into One Million in Real Estate in Your Spare Time by Ralph Nickerson. Before the group of 10 had finished the study of the fourth chapter I had read the whole book and purchased my first building. Twelve months later, I owned 26 units and the other nine study group members were still trying to finish the book. Being able to see opportunities and act decisively to seize them is important for succeeding in business.

You must be decisive as you lead your LearningRx center. The need to make decisions comes almost every day. You will succeed if you make a habit of gathering all the information you need and then acting without delay.

I know people who spend their whole lives hesitating. They put their dreams on hold. They watch the stock reports and try to catch the next big market wave. But they always end up delaying.

If you're not careful you can know the goal but find yourself unwilling to do what is needed to achieve it. Double your efforts to go ahead and take the plunge. Take the chance to make a decision—even if it means you'll need to correct your course later. That's so much better than sitting on the sidelines.

It's possible that your plans may turn out differently from how you'd hoped. But if you never put them into action they'll never turn out at all. To be an effective LearningRx franchisee, you must be decisive.

Too many people think so long over decisions that they end up never making any. I believe this is because many people aren't sure where they are going.

A Word of Caution

One caveat: Being decisive with almost no thinking is not smart.

A few years ago at a family picnic, my brother Bryan boasted that he could climb the 400-foot cliff in front of us. After a quick look at Bryan, who wasn't in good shape, and the cliff, which seemed almost straight up, I offered him a $1,000 if he could get to the top within 30 minutes. He quickly accepted my wager and started jogging to the cliff as his wife was screaming, "Bryan, stop, you'll kill yourself!"

At that moment I realized what a dumb, quick offer I'd just made. A true lose-lose proposition. Either Bryan was going to fall and kill himself—for which I would be blamed—or I was going to pay him $1,000! Either way I'd lose. As the family tore into me for making such a stupid offer and Bryan reached the halfway mark I yelled up a counter-offer: $500 if he would stop.

Bryan didn't stop and he made it to the top—so I gladly made out a $1,000 check to him on the spot. Though I blew it that time, that lesson of failing to think through the ramifications of a hasty decision has saved me from making two or three big mistakes since.

A second caveat: Be realistic.

This is illustrated by another wager the Gibson family often engages in—weight loss. My brother Robin, always optimistic and unrealistic about how much weight he can lose, is vulnerable to almost every challenge proposed. He fully believes he can achieve the loss but never does. It's important to accurately and realistically gauge a situation before coming to a quick decision.

But with those caveats in mind, realize that most people need to go ahead and take the plunge. Most people err on the side of not being decisive enough, not on the side of being hasty in their decisiveness.

Leonardo da Vinci wrote, "Iron rusts from disuse; water loses its purity from stagnation...even so does inaction sap the vigour of the mind."

Determination

The fourth characteristic of a successful franchisee is determination. You can't fail if your determination for success is strong enough. Here's another story from Kim that illustrates this:

> I had just graduated and was supporting my husband, who had a year left in college, but a part-time night job wasn't doing it. Minneapolis had put a freeze on interviewing teachers because they had to cut jobs, had no positions, and had thousands of applications on file.

On a call to my dad discussing how tough it was, I explained how I'd tried everything: called, stopped by schools, sent in résumés and applications, everything I knew.

He reminded me that Aristotle Onassis got his first job as a "ship's boy" by showing up every day for six months at the gate of the captain's home begging for a job. He suggested I do the same, "Go down there and park yourself in the superintendent's office and don't budge until the guy who makes the hiring decisions talks with you." Wow! People just don't do that! You can't force people to talk to you.

But I knew Dad was right—I don't have to be like everyone else. I had nothing to lose.

The next morning I was at the door as the janitor opened it; when the assistant arrived I told her I was there to see the person who hired teachers. When she asked if I had an appointment I told her, "No, I don't, but I've been waiting for one for the last five months." She replied, "Honey, we don't have any positions, we're not interviewing, and Dr. X has meetings all day. I'll find your application and put it on his desk and let him know you were here, so go home."

I wanted to turn around and leave, but I heard an inner voice say, "Be bold as a lion." I would wait. He arrived and walked by me a few times on the way to meetings as I sat there all day. Late in the afternoon he indicated he had two more meetings and that I should go home. I told him I'd wait.

About 6:30 he came out and told me I had five minutes. I jumped up, followed him, and shared my passion for teaching. "Well, you certainly are persistent," he said. "In my 30 years in education I've never seen someone as stubborn as you, especially after you were made to feel unwanted." He added that he had one job that had opened up that day, but I would be crazy to take it and he would be foolish to give it to me—a new teacher.

It was a fifth-grade class of emotionally disturbed students who had gone through three teachers in a month and a half, including a former principal, and he couldn't keep a sub in there past noon. I told him, "I'll take it!" I did—and had a great year—but that's another story.

Conclusion

Opening a LearningRx Center can feel a lot like knocking on an unknown door to talk to an unknown person. There are obstacles, closed doors, and hidden paths.

But it's much more enjoyable to be finding your path as a business owner than it is to stay on a safe but boring path in someone else's journey. Launching a business takes the kind of intestinal fortitude most people could never generate. It takes a hero.

And a hero always does what's right, even when it's hard. A hero confronts the challenges of this life.

He or she takes responsibility.

I admire you for stepping forth boldly while most people sit back and never pursue their dreams.

CHAPTER 4

Pursue Excellence

THERE IS A REASON LearningRx's programs are so powerful and unmatched. But it's not that we sat down one day and came up with the process in its perfected form. It is the result of 40 years of refining, the input from hundreds of contributors, and thousands of...you guessed it...changes.

In 1968, I started my quest to help students learn better. I was dyslexic, which meant that reading was always time-consuming and difficult for me. And yet I was motivated to make it easier for others. My desire to treat the causes of learning problems moved me to action. I decided I would follow the evidence no matter where it led, even if it led me away from my profession as a pediatric optometrist and into other fields of study.

This quest required me to challenge the long-held belief in the medical community that the brain is fixed at birth. First, I had to overcome my own training in this matter, and then

I had to be willing to accept years of ridicule from the medical community. Even today, many neuroscientists who themselves have proved that the brain is changeable nevertheless have a hard time believing that it can change as much as we have documented in our LearningRx programs.

I started my journey by training children's eyes to work better because I incorrectly assumed poor visual skills was the main issue behind most learning difficulties. But I soon learned that this wasn't good enough. Over time I added sensory-motor, visual and auditory processing, attention, memory, reasoning, and processing speed procedures.

Each addition created a change in learning. Each change added to our knowledge of how to achieve increased improvement in learning skills. What would we have gained if we'd decided that the first added procedure was enough? We would have achieved modest improvements but nothing like the gains we see now.

We made other changes, too. We began comparing test scores from before a student entered the program to after the student completed the program. We changed from working with one trainer per three students to one trainer per student. We added our loading techniques to escalate the enhancement achieved in each procedure.

In short, we did nothing but change, change, and change, always seeking the optimum procedures in each area. We never printed more manuals than the number of doctors attending our next seminar—because by the following seminar the manual would be changed.

Did it pay off?

It did. In 1985 we were achieving skill gains of 2 months for each month of training. A year later, after developing some tremendous breakthroughs in our training procedures, our average gains were almost 10 months of skill gains per month of training. That's an incredible 500 percent increase. We could have stopped there. But we've kept working to increase the program's effectiveness. Today, because of all our experimentation and refinement (i.e., *changes*), we have over 65 LearningRx centers across the country.

Yes, our commitment to making changes has certainly paid off.

Excellence Requires Reinvention

In business you must continuously reinvent yourself. You must cultivate a healthy dissatisfaction with the status quo, a creative uneasiness with "good enough." You must always seek refinements to enhance what you're doing.

How you're conducting business today may be good. It may, indeed, be the very best way to operate. But there's the possibility that a better way is out there waiting to be discovered. And you'll never know if there might be a better way if you don't go looking for it. To achieve excellence in any endeavor, be it sport or art or business, you must be willing to try new approaches and throw out old ones if something better presents itself.

In the context of LearningRx, you pursue excellence by continuously reinventing in two ways: reinventing yourself and reinventing systems and processes.

Reinvent Yourself

To lead your staff to excellence, you must set the example. You must put yourself on a path of continuous self-improvement. Make an effort to expand your knowledge by reading new books or attending seminars. Join business clubs that seek to cross-pollinate ideas by bringing together businesspeople from different industries. To create an environment of constant improvement, begin with yourself. There are many opportunities to do so.

When my son Shawn was in fourth grade we would walk four miles each morning while I drilled him in word math problems. A few months later he placed fourth in a state math competition. While traveling as a family, we spent much of the time playing mental games and listening to business tapes or stories of successful people. My daughter Kim recalls how this paid off for her:

> When we traveled, Dad was always playing tapes of books or seminars. The rest of the family would have preferred listening to something else, as Dad's tapes made us go to sleep. However, years later it was amazing how the things we had heard on those trips—even when we thought we were sleeping—helped us. In my first job interview after college, twice the answer to interview questions came straight from those tapes I'd heard years earlier. I couldn't believe it. And by the way, I got the job.

Such resources have helped me reinvent myself for a long time. I first became convinced that books would be of value beyond college when, in my second year of graduate school, a life insurance agent contacted me. Me, a lowly grad student! So of course I would meet with him. After all, wasn't buying life insurance a mark of adulthood?

Before the meeting I decided I needed to learn all I could about buying insurance. So I hit the public library. I learned I should buy term insurance and invest the difference I saved by not buying whole life. Years later, when I had a family and bought insurance, and even today, I'm buying term and investing the difference. I would not have learned that had I not read that book.

Reading pays. Even being dyslexic, I have read – on average – a book a week for the past 40 years.

You must cultivate a healthy dissatisfaction with the status quo, a creative uneasiness with "good enough".

I read for ideas, for underlying concepts that give me flashes of inspiration for my life or for business. Reading stimulates concepts I then try to apply. I'm constantly exploring new ideas.

You need to do this too. You reinvent yourself by being open to change in your thinking and doing business. This is how you achieve excellence.

Your business competitors are trying new ideas. Someone across town is implementing a better strategy right now, something that might begin to put a serious dent in your business. If you want to keep your franchise operating at its peak, you need to be up on the latest business thinking. You need to keep stretching yourself.

A constant reinvention of yourself will allow you not only to keep up with competitors but also to handle the challenges your center will face. Be willing to stop doing things the old way if that's pulling you down (within what is allowed in the Operations Manual, of course—but even then, if you have an improvement, let me know). Be willing to change how you operate on both a personal and professional level.

There is power in knowledge. Reading books and attending seminars can give you the advantage.

Reinventing yourself also allows you to make the most of what you have as a person. You have been given a number of talents. They are tools for you to use in the best way possible for as long as they're in your hands. You are a steward of your talents.

And you manage your talents wisely by constantly reinventing yourself.

Become a Time Expert

One of the best ways to reinvent yourself is to take control of your time. Because the misuse—or merely the unfocused use—of your time is a sure path to mediocrity in business.

The story is told of how Andrew Carnegie, steel magnate in the 1880s, learned this lesson. Carnegie hired a young management consultant to help increase the productivity of the office staff. After almost a month of observing the staff work, the consultant went into Mr. Carnegie's office with his recommendation. He said that most of the people wasted time getting started. It was as if they weren't sure what needed to be done and in what order. He suggested that before people went home in the evening, they should write down what needed to be done tomorrow and to prioritize their importance and, in the morning, start with number one.

Mr. Carnegie didn't expect such a simple solution and really questioned the value of the idea. The consultant suggested that Mr. Carnegie try it for a month and at the end of that time to send him a check for whatever he thought the idea was worth. The results were so dramatic that Mr. Carnegie sent him a check for $25,000. That was a lot of money more than 100 years ago.

Good time management equates to good life management. Especially when it comes to business, doing the right things in the right order is the path to excellence.

Where do you want to be in five years? Pretend that's a destination on a map. Now plot out the course between here and there. What are the major milestones you'll need to reach on your journey? What's the first thing you'll need to do, achieve, or learn to start approaching those markers?

Break down that journey into five chunks, one for each year between now and your five-year goal. Give yourself an annual project. Every year you concentrate on that portion of the trek.

Maybe this year, your goal is to get a better grip on how to do business in today's economy. So perhaps your project for this year is to start reading one business book per month. Maybe you decide you need to learn how to sell better, so your project is to seek out the top salespeople in the country and attend their seminars or buy their CD series. Maybe you determine that this year you need to learn how to manage money better, so you give yourself the project of taking courses in business finance.

Map out your course. Divide the journey into segments. Give yourself projects that achieve the goal for each segment. And make steady progress toward your goal.

You want a trick for knowing whether you're truly learning any material you're studying? Pretend that you will be teaching a class on it at the end of the year. Let's say your local community college has asked you to lead a seminar on this topic and you need to give your students mastery of the content. When you know you'll be teaching others, you'll definitely apply yourself to learn it. You never know what question some bright student might ask.

Good time management equates to good life management. Especially when it comes to business, doing the right things in the right order is the path to excellence.

And who knows? At the end of the year maybe you *could* teach a course on it. Or maybe you'll write it up as a business e-book and sell it online.

Have you heard of the 80/20 rule? It's an idea that applies to many realms of life. 80 percent of your success will result from 20 percent of your efforts. 80 percent of your income will come from 20 percent of your prospects.

The rule holds true when it comes to time management. That's why you need to follow the advice Andrew Carnegie received and make sure you're doing the main things first. You want your best time spent on the things that have the potential to earn you the most return.

How much time per week are you spending in the most important activities? This is where possibilities become paychecks. And this is where you need to be spending your time and energies. You can hire other people to do just about everything else.

In order to know what things you need to be doing and what

things to delegate to others, do some simple math. Figure out how much money you'd like to make in salary for a year. Then divide that by the number of business hours in a year. That gives you an hourly rate. Let's say you want to earn $80,000 a year in salary. When you divide that by 2,000 business hours, you get a rate of $40 per hour.

What tasks at your center must be done by someone who should be paid $40 per hour? Not many. For your center, that's doing face-to-face marketing with professionals—and the consultations. The other stuff can be done by employees who make less than $40 per hour. You need to be spending most of your time doing the things only you can do.

Begin by making a resolution right now. Say, "I resolve that from now on..." and fill in the blank. I resolve that from now on I will read a book a week, or concentrate on consultations, or hire someone to do the things that can be purchased for less than my hourly rate.

One final note about being a time expert: be on time. Promptness and punctuality are traits that you should hold in high regard. Do you hate waiting on someone when you're on time and the other person is late? Guess what? The other person will hate it if you're late. If six people are sitting around waiting for the seventh to arrive, the cost of that waiting isn't just 15 minutes—but rather 90 minutes' worth of salaries. Treat others the way you like to be treated.

Being on time shows respect and honor to others. Although patience is an honorable character trait, and you will no doubt get many opportunities to practice it, try not to inflict it on others. Be on time.

Reinventing Your Systems

The LearningRx franchisee system is on a path of constant self-reinvention. That means you will occasionally find that certain processes within your center will need to be changed as we continue to improve our practices to stay ahead.

When we think about the processes utilized in the centers, we keep one rule in mind: the new way must help us get the job done *better, for less money, and with fewer errors.*

I know it may be difficult to accept changes when we announce them from the home office. The ideas will be new to you and you won't have had the chance to play with them, experiment, find the right balance, and generally live with the new ideas for months, as we have. But I assure you that every change we implement will be for the purpose of helping you better do what you're doing, more cost effectively, and more precisely. For you, this means a better bottom line.

At LearningRx we value creativity. We recruit people with it and develop it in the people we have. The ability to think creatively is a gift, and we are determined to use it to the fullest. We welcome you and your staff's creativity as well. With our combined creativity we'll question the status quo and brainstorm processes to better maximize potential or solve problems.

Continuing to improve the system is critical to success. So for the sake of our franchise system and your own center, be open and embrace change and improvement. Commit to reinventing your processes constantly.

Conclusion

We are always in the process of renewal. Our skin cells and hair and brain cells are constantly regenerating. Moving to a new city or beginning a new business can give us the opportunity to reinvent ourselves, to become who we've always wanted to be.

The practice of challenging the status quo ensures that you will always be moving to a stronger, more robust situation. You don't want change just for the sake of change, of course. But by testing your assumptions and toying with radical new ideas and investigating new concepts, you're able to adapt and thrive. In the volatile financial environment in which we find ourselves, the ability to transform and upgrade is vital.

When it comes to maximizing a LearningRx franchise, *a* process is not necessarily *the* process. Even the best process can be improved upon. Commit yourself to the path of excellence, the path on which you are constantly seeking a better way.

SECTION 2

Strategies
Introduction to Section 2

THERE'S AN OLD QUOTE that says, "Sow an act and you reap a habit; sow a habit and you reap a character; sow a character and you reap a destiny."

Section 2 of this book is about doing the things that will reap a positive destiny for your LearningRx franchise. Here, I talk about the strategies and actions that engender good habits, strengthen character, and result in a positive destination. We'll look at vision, team building, and serving.

Your beliefs determine your values. Did you know that? If you believe it's going to turn cold next week, suddenly the value you place on fixing the furnace will go way up. In the same way, your values help generate your strategies. You want to orchestrate your center so that the values you hold will be acted out in your business. Your strategies then determine your behaviors, and your behaviors have consequences.

The most important consequence of your behaviors is that you become what you do.

So turn the page and let's get to work discovering the strategies and actions that will turn you and your franchise into what you've dreamed of.

CHAPTER 5

Have a Vision

A WORD FROM my daughter Tanya:

Every Monday or the day after a holiday there is a sense of anticipation and some anxiety at the LearningRx home office—because my dad's had a few days to come up with a new idea or project for us.

Others wander through life not sure where they're going, but not Dad—he's always thinking years ahead. We were raised to think ahead. Since I was a child, every January 1st we'd all sit down together and reveal our one- and five-year goals for different areas of our life. Years before Dad ever needed them, he set up business entities and structures. He planned his retirement 10 years before he retired at age 48.

But he couldn't remain retired; there were more visions to pursue. He was way ahead of his professional peers in developing therapies and business systems. He is a genius at seeing seemingly unrelated factors and synthesizing them into something new. When he held political office, he headed almost every study committee. His preschools were so effective that a local school official figured he must be mentally abusing children.

In 1980, before the first IBM personal computer, we packed up the car with five Apple clones and traveled the country teaching other medical professionals the value of computers in their offices. Even before the Apple, when we used to load software using cassettes, local TV stations would come to our home to do stories of the future use of computers in education and the home.

When Dad developed his first brain-training software program, there was only one other in existence. Unfortunately, he wasn't able to raise the funds for production, but those development companies he approached saw the future my Dad saw and used his ideas to create their own.

The ReadRx program is the result of Dad seeing how to take some current reading programs and making them far more effective. He even wrote to the companies, offering to help them improve their programs, but they turned him down. So Dad, Dean, and I created ReadRx (which has been statistically proven to be at least twice as effective as the next—best program). I could keep going on and on. But I think you get the idea: Vision is a strong suit of LearningRx.

There is power in vision. If one person casts a vision and many people catch it, everything can be changed.

What's Your Vision?

People will join you in your LearningRx quest if they believe in your vision. If they like what you're doing and feel it brings great benefit, they will partner with you in it.

You joined the LearningRx world because you believed in what it could do, right? You desire to come to the aid of people who are struggling. That's where you start: with a compelling vision that stirs the passion within you. Your vision tells people who you are, where you're going, and what drives your behavior.

What is your vision? Can you articulate it?

You need to practice doing so, because it is in communicating your vision—to staff, trainers, and customers—that you bring people on board with you. Not only should you be able to express your vision at the drop of a hat, you ought to write it out and publish it somehow, perhaps by having it written up by a calligrapher and hung in your reception room.

When you are passionate about your vision, your people will be too. You will involve them in your own crusade and thus gain their commitment. Your vision is the thing that takes people from where they are and gets them to another, better place they can glimpse because of you. Vision is a view of a desired future. It gives direction. Vision clarifies choices and makes decisions easy.

Vision is the heads-up (as if to listen) part of your leadership for your center. Implementation of that vision is the heads-down (as if to get to work) part of your leadership.

To implement your vision you need to set priorities and goals.

Set Priorities

Priorities determine your direction and measure your progress.

A business that is more about profit than value to the customer or employee will suffer the consequences of its priorities. But a business that prioritizes value to the customer or employee has things set up right, and the drive for profit is in its proper place. Tanya illustrates this with the following story:

> When I graduated from college I moved to Florida to start the first non-doctor-run cognitive training program. Although at the time Dad was partially retired, he helped me get started. I followed his instruction and soon had my first enrollment.
>
> Dad was watching my first session, which wasn't going well because the 15-year-old didn't really want to be there. After a few minutes, Dad stepped in and took over the training. He tried everything he could to get the boy to cooperate, without success. He then asked me for the $2,300 check that, minutes before, I had received from the boy's mother and put aside for safekeeping. He took that check and returned it to the boy's mother.
>
> I couldn't believe it. My first earnings! I had worked so hard for that first student and first check. Dad gave it back and told the student, "When you're ready to work

hard and make good use of your mom's money, give me a call." As the student left, Dad said, "Tanya, you have just paid for one of the most valuable lessons you'll ever learn. Someday you will teach it to others. Doing what is right is worth far more than any profit."

Although it was a tough lesson then, he was right and I've taught it to hundreds since then.

> If one person casts a vision, and many people catch it, everything can be changed.

My son-in-law, Wayne (Kim's husband), recently delivered a sermon that illustrated how to set priorities. As visual aids he used a large jar and different-sized stones. He showed that if you start by placing the large 3-inch stones into the jar, followed by the 1-inch stones and then sand to fill in the spaces between the large stones, you can fill the jar. But if you start with the sand and then add the small stones, you won't be able to get in all the large stones. The lesson is this: concentrate first on the biggest priorities and the lesser priorities will fall into place.

The 80/20 rule says the same thing. You're a 20-percenter if:

- You understand that of all the things on your list of 37 things to do, six or seven of them are more important than all the other items put together. The 80-percenter acts as though all items are equally important.

- You are profoundly selective about the information you read, listen to, and act upon. The 80-percenter will listen to almost everything.

• You're an independent thinker. You know that more often than not the masses are tragically wrong. The 80-percenter is the masses. While you're smiling, the 80-percenter is complaining—80 percent of the time.

You need to be in that top 20 percent. It's like the story about the two guys being chased by the bear. One says to the other, "I don't have to outrun the bear; I just have to outrun you." You need to outrun the 80 percent, especially in tough times—which I know you can do if you're a 20-percenter.

According to the 80/20 rule, 20 percent of businesses will take advantage of the good times and the bad. Be a 20-percenter. *Carpe Diem*—seize the day. And in bad times, make sure the bear seizes someone else.

Set Goals

Successful franchisees are invariably goal-oriented. They have a clear idea of what they want to accomplish and how they plan to do it. They have written down their goals and they refer to them regularly.

Does this sound like you? If it doesn't, can you form this habit and make it part of your everyday activities? I believe you can.

In my first year out of college, I listened to a tape series by Paul J. Meyer, a pioneer of the personal development industry. Meyer emphasized the importance of setting goals for these five areas of your life: social, spiritual, physical, mental, and financial. That year I sat down and came up with a one-year and five-year goal in each of those areas, and every year since I've done so again.

As Tanya mentioned earlier, we now make it a family activity. On New Year's Eve we each create these five goals for ourselves, and throughout the year we hold each other accountable. It's amazing how many of our goals we have realized. One goal remains elusive, however. Although some of us have climbed Pikes Peak, others in the Gibson clan have had little success with our physical goals. But we haven't given up.

What are your goals? What change would you like to see in your life in one year in the social realm? What about in the spiritual? The physical? The mental? Or the financial? Go ahead and write down those goals.

Then write a plan for how you are going to accomplish each one. Studies have shown that those who write down their goals accomplish significantly more than those who do not.

And how do you achieve your goals? You break them down into bite-sized tasks.

Which reminds me of a story. Can you eat a car? It seems impossible, right? But it has been done. Dick Miller ate a 2,800-pound automobile. How? By eating one small piece at a time. It took him more than five years, but he did it.

Small tasks are how you achieve your goals. Goals are how you implement your priorities. Goals and priorities together are how you implement your vision.

Conclusion

Vision is critical, but you can't stop with vision. Vision gets people going, but it's abstract and theoretical. It needs to be brought to earth and made practical. That's where you enter the realm of priorities and goals. These are how you translate a high-sounding vision into reality.

Your center needs all of the above. It needs the vision you provide as leader. It also needs priorities and goals from its leader. Everyone needs to be on board with the direction you're going and the impulse that drives the entire venture. In later chapters we'll help you develop specific plans to reach your vision.

CHAPTER 6

Select & Maximize Your Staff

THE SINGING GROUP *Celtic Woman* has a great song on their *A New Journey* CD. The song "At the Ceili" tells of three young women who go to a big dance hoping to find romance.

Through the course of the song, one of the women finds herself being pursued by two likely candidates: one handsome but poor and the other rich but not as thrilling to her heart. She sings about her dilemma. She has no wish to live a life of dishwashing and poverty, but neither does a wealthy but loveless life entice her.

In the end she determines to marry the poor man. Better to have love than riches, she says. If you have love, then perhaps riches will come and perhaps they will not, but you'll always have the wealth of your intertwined hearts. But to have wealth without love is no life at all.

Choosing Your Staff

Selecting the employees who will staff your LearningRx center is a little like this song. You won't be choosing between wealthy and poor candidates, probably, but you will often have a choice.

On the one hand you will have candidates with an impressive skill-set but possibly a lousy attitude. Their résumés may sparkle but you get the sense that they're not exactly eager to serve you or your center. On the other hand, you'll have candidates with perhaps a lower skill-set and very little experience, but with a wonderful attitude. They don't know the first thing about training or customer relations or how to answer the phone, but they're eager to learn and serve.

Which should you choose? The first one, with those great skills, would get you ahead right out of the gate. The other would be a "project" and wouldn't necessarily be a positive contributor for awhile.

I would advise you to marry the poor man. Go with the candidate who has the great attitude.

Skills can be taught, but a servant's heart does not usually develop over time. No matter how long the runway, a pig will never learn to fly. Better to go with the person of higher character than the person with a better résumé, if indeed you must make that choice.

Although I know you are a very capable businessperson, you can't do everything. Your center will require more work than any one person can do. Since your business hinges on serving customers and meeting their needs, you'll need help doing that. What you accomplish depends on the people you gather around you.

It's important to find people who complement your gifts and abilities. Having an employee with exactly the same skill set as yours won't provide you the talents you aren't as strong in. Look for someone who can complement you and bring in the skills needed in your center.

As a good leader, you should always be looking for talented people to join your organization. Such people multiply your effectiveness and help you achieve your goals. Conversely, if you select your staff poorly it can have staggering consequences: lost time, declining performance, missed opportunities, and lowered morale.

To fill your staff you're going to conduct employment interviews. You're going to sit down with a candidate and have a talk while you determine whether this person would be an asset for your center.

When you conduct an interview, be on the lookout for a willingness to serve, a warm personality, a sharp mind, and, if interviewing for a trainer position, whether you would want this person training your own child.

I've already touched on the importance of the first one, a willingness to serve, but I want to emphasize it again. Without that, none of the rest will matter and you'll find yourself wishing you hadn't hired that person.

Toward the end of the interview, if you like what you see in this potential employee, encourage the candidate to interview *you*. What questions does this person have about you, your style, or what you're hoping to achieve through the center?

An interview isn't just about finding good people, after all. It's about you and the candidate determining together whether this would be a beneficial alliance for both parties. You want your employees to feel they are in a place where they can thrive, help people, make a difference, and make a decent income. A satisfied employee is a tremendous asset to your center.

With every pair of hands you hire, you get a free brain. So use it!

Placing Your Staff

When you hire someone you probably have a good idea of where you want to place him or her. You've got a need at the front desk or you need trainers or someone to do assessments.

That's all as it should be. But when it comes to where you've placed an employee, don't let your first decision necessarily be your final decision. You may find that this person has strengths that would make him or her even more effective in another role at your center.

One of the ramifications of our business model is the need for many part-time trainers with college degrees. This pool has produced many of our center administrators and almost a third of our home office staff. Working with your employees at a center gives you a wonderful opportunity to see people up close over time and get to know their capabilities and attitudes. Perhaps you've got a future administrator working for you now.

It's always better to fit people into their right positions

rather than leaving them in a position that doesn't play to their strengths. If you don't put them where they should be, you may have to come along and fix a mess later. Plugging the right people into the right spots is a great way to make your center thrive and your staff morale soar.

Now we come back to the choice in the *Celtic Woman* song. If you've picked employees with great attitudes and high character you'll be able to find the right spots for them and they'll take to your training and instruction well. Working with moldable employees like that is always better than choosing inflexible people who might be good at one thing but aren't willing to serve, change, or fully engage with your goals.

Engage Your Staff

Your staff can reach their goals (and help you attain yours) only when they are fully engaged with your vision.

You want buy-in from your staff. You want them to partner with you in your cause, your work, your mission, and even in yourself as leader. It starts by hiring people with the right attitude and it continues by putting those people in the right roles. But don't forget your employees' *minds*. With every pair of hands you hire you get a free brain thrown into the bargain. So use it!

Enabling each member of your team to play a meaningful role will generate a wonderful climate and an infectious energy. Those things will, in turn, help the organization fulfill its shared mission.

Let your staff know that you value them. You do this when you listen, invest time, and show you care about them. Author

John Maxwell says, "People will not give you their hand until they see your heart." Let your staff know that you value your relationship with each one of them.

Value Your Staff

When you see your staff engaged and working hard in the right roles you'll naturally feel inclined to praise them. If those praises don't come naturally to you, then you need to cultivate the ability to appreciate others in demonstrative ways.

You want to set up your staff to win. This means recognizing each worker's potential, dignity, and worth. An employee who does something for you out of mere obedience or following a rule is operating at the lowest level of relationship with you. Master and slave, almost. That's not exactly setting the person up to succeed. But if you communicate to your employees that you're all about keeping their best interests at heart, they will follow you willingly. You'll raise your level of relationship and gain the buy-in you need to succeed. So let your employees know that their success is important to you, too.

When I ran my practice, I'd often start my day with three pennies in my right pocket. Each time I praised a different staff member I could move one coin to the other pocket. My mission was to get them all into my left pocket by the end of the day.

If you want your staff to buy in to your mission you must become a servant to the people you lead. That means submitting yourself to them and treating them as valuable and important. That means praising them and setting aside your own self-importance to humbly serve them. A servant's heart can be developed but it takes a conscious choice. Dean is our chief operating officer and also my son-in-law. He lives this. He is constantly helping staff members move beds, couches, or a whole house full of furniture. And that example has spread so that if anyone needs a wall painted, a garage cleaned, or a car repaired, you would find other staff members there helping.

When you recognize and appreciate the efforts of your staff, they feel valued. They feel like an important part of your mission. Psychologically they ally themselves with you more fully and buy into your center that much more. This note received from a staff member illustrates this point:

> *Dear Ken & Dean,*
>
> *I have wanted to write to you for quite some time. Thank you for blessing me and my children beyond any words. From the day of my interview, when because of a snowstorm I needed to bring my children with me— and you offered them lunch, coloring books, toys, and movies—I've been amazed at the grace and generosity you have offered to me.*
>
> *Now, two years later and after the many days when my kids have ended up at work with me for one reason or another, I continue to experience the value you place on family and am so grateful for the safe and non-judgmental environment you provide to us.*
>
> *I love working at LearningRx because of it and it makes me want to help out even more wherever needed.*

I could not imagine a better family work environment to help balance my life and raise my kids! Thank you, thank you, and thank you.

Share Your Values, Vision, and Maybe Even Your Books

Talk to your employees about the values you hold personally and for LearningRx. Letting them in on your perspective creates bonding and fills the center with a feeling of meaningful common purpose.

Especially emphasize that the team is there for the primary purpose of maximizing the abilities of the students. When their cognitive abilities are maximized, their lives will be enriched. That's a motivating goal for your team. Keeping that before their eyes will make it easy for them to commit and to give their best.

To that end, since the mid-1980s I've always opened our financial books. I've felt my full-time staff would have better buy-in if they were in the know, seeing and understanding that profit comes from increasing income and controlling expenses. And since I was sharing the profit with them, rather than hoarding it, I had nothing to hide.

The only expense items I've kept confidential are salaries. I've found that no matter how much I want to believe that my staff could understand why their pay may be lower than another's, most times the human trait of self-interest arises and creates problems, so individual staff pay is kept secret.

Conclusion

Your franchise will succeed only to the degree that your staff succeeds. Every leader needs competent followers whose morale is high and who are engaged in the leader's vision.

You gather this kind of staff around you by becoming a servant leader who aspires to greatness only in the sense of being great in serving. You do it by looking for the right things in your candidates during the interview process. You gain this kind of staff by placing your employees in positions that maximize their strengths. And you create this kind of staff by engaging them in your vision, praising them, and valuing their relationships and results.

The Celtic Woman song talked about choosing a poor man for love over a rich man for comfort. Select your staff well— develop them and serve them—and you may end up with the best of both worlds.

CHAPTER 7

Serve Others

THERE'S A SCENE in the movie *We Were Soldiers* that has stuck with me. In it, American soldiers are training before being deployed to fight in Vietnam. One of the would-be leaders among the men chews out his troops and leads them in valiant, gung-ho charges, seeking glory. Another of the leaders kneels on the ground before his guys and helps one with a boot that's hurting his foot. Our hero looks at this second man and proclaims him a true leader, one whom men would follow into anything.

There's something incredible about servant leaders. It almost goes against logic to think that someone willing to stoop to serve those under him would be a more effective leader than someone shouting for obedience. And yet we've seen it true in our lives. When those in authority genuinely care about us we find it easy to be loyal to them. We respect those leaders who have respected us.

This is a lesson I've had to learn. Servant leadership doesn't come naturally to me. Back in the 1970s, I joined a multi-level networking company. I believed in the product and was a zealous worker. I received the Pacesetter of the Year Award in my first year and went on in the second to win the President's Award as the company's top recruiter.

But that's where my rapid growth hit an obstacle. Recruiting is all well and good, but it brings with it something I wasn't so good at: mentoring. These new recruits needed hand-holding and instruction and encouragement. But those weren't things I was naturally suited to give. Why couldn't they just go out and do it instead of complaining about it? Why couldn't they simply catch the vision and figure out for themselves how to reach their goals?

Needless to say, support isn't my strong suit. Even today I need a crew of team members around me who can offer hand-holding to those who need it. I'm not the most patient or tactful, even now. However, that doesn't mean I haven't learned how important servant leadership is. I'm learning to enact it not only in my own life but throughout the structure of LearningRx.

In order for you to succeed as a LearningRx franchisee, you will need to become a servant leader, too. You will need to be the leader who helps those under you who are experiencing difficulty—or they won't follow you anywhere, least of all to success. And you won't get there, either.

What Is Servant Leadership?

Before you can do it, you must understand it. The key to becoming a leader who is followed is to understand what servant leadership is. In my definition, *service is investing in the development and well-being of others for the common good.*

Perhaps you can see the usefulness of this definition right away. Whom do you serve as a LearningRx franchisee? You serve the people of your community—the students going through the program and their families—and you serve your employees. You also serve the LearningRx system, but our focus here will be on how you serve those under you.

> *Your influence is determined by the degree to which you place other people's interests before your own.*

So how do you invest in the development and well-being of these groups? Let's take them one at a time.

Serving Your Customers

Keep in mind that your LearningRx franchise business is not about selling. It's not about getting people to buy programs so you can pay the bills and make a profit. Your business is about meeting the needs of your customers. It's about serving them.

If that's true, then everything you do should be pointed to that goal. Every decision you make needs to go back to the question: "Will this better serve my customer?" If the answer is no, you might want to reconsider it.

What does the perfect LearningRx center look like? When you let your mind dare to envision the ultimate LearningRx experience, both for your students and for their families, what do you imagine? What does it feel like? What do the entry areas look like? The front desk? The lighting? The consultation rooms?

The training stations? The decorations? The bathrooms? How is a customer family taken through the process—in the best of all scenarios?

Let that perfect vision be your goal. Hire staff with that goal in mind. Choose music and chairs and light bulbs with that vision set before you. Set your operating hours with that goal in mind. Make it easy for customers to do business with you. Establish your director of first impressions' phone greeting with that perfect experience in view. Have multiple payment plans. Imagine the ultimate consultation scene playing out before you, then take steps to make that vision a reality.

Make doing business with you a warm and pleasant experience for your customer. Train your staff to be attentive, friendly, and knowledgeable so your customers feel they're receiving good value for their money. Offer free coffee, kind greetings, and clean restrooms. Make customers feel happy to come back—and to refer others.

Some people hear what I'm suggesting and think, "How can I possibly afford to do this?" Much of what I'm talking about can seem like frivolous extras, things you can maybe add in a year or two after you see how well this center is going to do. But my question to you is, how can you afford *not* to do this? How do you think you're going to make it a year or two if you haven't served your customer from Day 1 by making it a pleasant experience?

One caveat here: The customer isn't always right. Now, in the sense that you always give honor and respect to your customers, the adage is true. But in actual practice, it's not.

Sometimes your customer may ask for something you're

not inclined to give. Maybe a customer thinks you should have Starbucks® coffee in your reception room or that you should offer professional psychological counseling as part of your program. Maybe a customer thinks you should move your offices or stay open on Sundays—or do any of a hundred other things that are outside your vision or values.

Sometimes you have to ignore what your customers want. You can't please everyone. You need to look after the needs of your customer, certainly, but only within the limits of your vision.

Still, the idea that you are serving your customer should always remain in your mind. Your thoughts and actions should always be focused on how you can better invest in their development and well-being for the common good.

Serving Your Staff

As a LearningRx franchisee, your primary area of leadership is not actually the customer. It's your employees. The servant's work you do for your staff directly impacts how your customers are treated, so by extension you are serving both groups when you serve your employees. But you'll be spending many more hours with those you hire than with customers who walk in the door.

How do you serve your staff? The same way you serve your customers: by imagining the ideal workplace environment and striving to bring it about. By working to help the soldier with the painful boot, figuratively speaking. By respecting your people.

Your employees will look after customers the same way you look after them. By caring for your staff you will model the kind of care you want them to extend to customers.

I don't like imposing a lot of rules on the home office staff. I think rules are mainly created to keep staff members "in line." Indeed, most rules were created because one time someone did something unwise and now there has to be a rule in place because of that person's failing. In my opinion, it would be better to remove the person than add a rule. More on that idea in a minute.

Having said that, though, there are two guidelines I recommend for every LearningRx center: the circle and the no-nattering rule.

Guideline 1: The Circle

See the diagram below. The circle is divided into three equal parts, like a "peace" symbol. The slices of the pie are labeled with the words: "agreement," "caring," and "communication."

These three pieces are vital components of serving your staff. Agreement means each staff person is working together toward LearningRx's vision, mission, and goals. Caring refers to each staff person's compassion toward fellow staff members.

Communication refers to the open line of discussion with other employees.

All three pieces must be working together for your center's staff to operate as it should. Each piece must be cherished and nurtured. Because if we aren't in agreement with what our roles are and how we operate, we soon stop communicating with each other, and then we'll stop caring. Or if we stop caring about each other, we'll stop communicating, and very quickly we'll get out of agreement. If we stop communicating, both caring and agreement will suffer.

Working together at LearningRx ought to be fun. Life is too short to have a job you don't enjoy. You serve your employees by making the circle complete, by making sure all pieces of it are functioning as they should.

Periodically stop for 10 minutes to deliberately think about how these three elements are working—or not working—in your center. What could you do to strengthen the piece that may be slipping? Keep the pieces working and the whole wheel will roll along smoothly.

Guideline 2: No Nattering

One thing that will get in the way of a successful LearningRx franchise is negative chatter. Nattering. Harmful gossip. Nattering will lead to a quick demise of morale and customer service.

Sometimes serving your staff means removing someone from the staff. If you have someone who cannot be consistently positive, he or she has to go. For the sake of the team.

This is never fun. I once had to deal with this in the case of a close relative who worked for me. His work performance was exceptional but his constant complaints just seemed to poison the team environment. After numerous one-on-one sessions with him in which I tried to correct the situation, I finally had to end the work relationship. (It's almost impossible to correct a consistently negative person, but we did try.) It was not an enjoyable experience. However, soon after his departure the work day and the workplace became enjoyable again, and in the following six months we had our greatest period of growth.

If you find yourself with a natterer, you may need to let that person go.

Incidentally, be sure you don't natter, either. Nothing kills employees' enjoyment of their job like a negative boss.

As I said before, I don't like a lot of rules. However, the circle and the no-nattering guidelines will help you serve your employees and help make your LearningRx center a joyful place.

More Tools for Serving Your Staff

Our definition of service is *investing in the development and well-being of others for the common good.* The ideas above for serving your customer and serving your staff will set you on the path to investing in the well-being of those around you. The following additional ideas will help you serve your staff even better:

- In disagreements or areas of perceived conflict, seek first to understand your employees. Only then should you seek to be understood. Your staff must feel listened to. That's a big part of how you respect them.

- Celebrate the achievement of your employees. Value their potential.

- Make your decisions openly and, when possible, in consultation with your staff.

- Hand out personal evaluations—of you! Let your employees help you see your blind spots. Use these evaluations as a means to improve the overall performance of your center. Because that's the goal, isn't it? Don't a happy staff and a well-functioning center trump the false feeling that you can do no wrong?

It sounds counterintuitive, but when you place the importance of others above your own importance, you are almost always the one to reap the rewards. That's not your motive, of course; it's simply how things tend to work out. If you want to become great, you must humble yourself and serve. LearningRx continues to be an organization known for its servant spirit, and that should be an important characteristic of your center.

Conclusion

As a franchisee you must be involved in what each of your team members is doing and becoming. You must learn to serve your employees in the ways suggested above. You must become attuned to how the work environment you're creating is contributing to that process.

Also pay attention to how your *customer* is experiencing the workplace environment you've created. Serving your customer and your staff will result in you successfully investing in the development and well-being of others for the common good.

An effective LearningRx franchisee is a server.

When you are a server to your customers and staff, they will follow you. They will follow you into success and an environment of mutual advantage.

SECTION 3

Profitability
Introduction to Section 3

IN THE MID-1980s, I opened six eye-care centers in six months.

I was a real entrepreneur. But something wasn't right. Between my six practices, a practice-management software business, and trading stock options, I was over my head in demands and chaos. My finances were out of control and I had no idea what was going wrong.

I was so desperate for help that when I received a cold call one day from someone offering to sell me a $12,000 program to learn how to control my business, I bought it.

But it saved my business. If it hadn't have been for the pain and confusion I was in I never would've reached out for the help I needed. That program started me on the path that taught me how to manage my business by *objectives*. And in this section I'm going to teach you many of those lessons—for significantly less than $12,000.

Managing by Checkbook

Most small businesses manage their finances the way families do: by using the checkbook balance. If there's money in the bank, they make expenditures. If there isn't money in the bank, they don't.

Managing by checkbook is the reason 40 percent of Americans 55 and older have less than $100,000 saved toward retirement. It's why fewer than 2 percent of my 250 management clients in the early 1990s knew what percentage of their income was going to staff salaries.

Hardly any small businesses ever review their finances on a profit and loss statement—except at tax time—and even fewer study their balance sheet.

Listen, your checkbook won't tell you what's going on with the finances in your business. If you have a low balance in your checkbook, what does it mean?

- It could mean you don't have enough customers

- It could mean your expenses are too high

- It could mean you're not collecting enough of what's owed you

- It could mean your prices are too low (or, in LearningRx terminology, that your average case size is too small)
- It could mean someone is embezzling from you
- Or it could mean you've got too many boats!

The point is that you simply can't know, not by just looking at what you have in your bank account. Your checkbook might tell you that you *have* a problem—but not what's *causing* it.

Keys to Profitability

You need to learn, as I did, how to manage not by the checkbook but by objectives.

You may know how to market, how to sell, how to balance your checkbook, how to provide your services well, and more, but none of that means you know how to manage your business for a profit.

Since that day in the mid-1980s I've learned some terrific principles for business profitability. In the following chapters, I'll give you 15 keys that will help you walk with clarity in areas of finances where so many others stumble in the dark.

CHAPTER 8

Profitability Keys 1- 4:

Manage Your Center's Key Areas with Objectives & Stats

THERE'S A STORY ABOUT an American technology company that outsourced some of its manufacturing to a Japanese factory. In the specifications, the American company stipulated that they would accept three defective parts per 10,000.

When the first shipment arrived, it came with a letter from the Japanese company: "We sometimes have a hard time understanding American business practices. However, in the 10,000 units of your shipment please find the three defective ones packaged separately. We had them specially manufactured to meet your order."

Sometimes it's not easy to know if you're meeting with the kind of success you're wanting. Misunderstandings, unclear directives, and a failure to communicate can leave you wondering if you're getting closer to your destination.

In my years of business I have discovered several keys to

success. They will help you know where you're headed, how to get there, and, perhaps most importantly, how to know if you're making progress. In this chapter we will talk about the first four of these keys.

The first one is to define your center's key operating functions. The second is to create objectives for each of these functions. The third key is to determine how to measure your success in achieving those objectives. And the fourth key is to be sure each activity is specifically assigned to someone.

Let's talk about each one in turn.

Key #1: Identify Your Main Functions

Your center is unique in many ways. You bring your own style and personality to it and it is tempered by your location, clientele, and even the building in which it operates.

However, there are many aspects of operating your center that you have in common with every other center and most other businesses. These are your core operating functions. They are the areas of executive, financial, operations, marketing, sales, product, and quality control.

- The executive function of your center is the leadership part. The planning, the strategy, and the managerial concerns.

- The financial function involves the inflow and outflow of money. This is where you collect money, pay bills, and crunch the numbers.

- The operations function refers to your facilities and staff.

It's where you make sure you have what you need to
provide the services of LearningRx.

- The marketing purpose is to make your center more widely
known among potential customers.

- The sales function is the part of your business in which
you persuade people to purchase the services you provide.

- The products function refers to the services you offer. It's
the thing of value you provide in exchange for payment.

- The quality control function is where you evaluate all of
the above so you can get a good handle on how well your
business is doing and how positively or negatively your
clients perceive your services.

Unlike those American businessmen, your definition of success
is not supplying three defective units for every 10,000. You define
success in your center by making demonstrable progress in each
of these areas. The first step toward achieving success with your
franchise is identifying what belongs in each of these categories.

The next step is creating a growth plan for each one.

Key #2: Create Objectives for Each Key Area

If your business is defined by the key areas we just discussed,
then it follows that success in your business is achieved by seeing
success in each of those areas.

The next key is to come up with objectives for each of these
crucial areas. What do you want to achieve in these spheres?

Here's an example of possible objectives:

- *Executive*—To create an expanding, productive, and viable organization

- *Financial*—To collect all fees, pay all bills, increase cash flow, and reduce debt

- *Operations*—To have an inviting facility and enthusiastic, productive, and efficient staff

- *Marketing*—To expand the number of prospective students

- *Sales*—To increase the number of students committed to and excited about starting their training

- *Products*—To significantly improve students' cognitive skills and reading

- *Quality Control*—To provide high-quality care and perceived value

What are your objectives going to be? What do you want your marketing to look like? What about your facilities and staff? Accounts receivable? Take time to modify my suggested objectives to come up with objectives that are right for you.

I have found that when I don't know how I'm doing in any one key area that is the area I'm likely failing in. You need to watch all of these parts of your business. You need to determine objectives and then set goals for each area so you'll know how well you are doing.

And you do that best by making these objectives *measurable*.

Key #3: Determine How to Measure Success in Your Plan

How will you know if you're making progress in those crucial areas? You need to determine how you're going to measure how successful you are at meeting those objectives.

You do this by *defining the stats* and *measuring them monthly*.

Here's an example of possible stats for the key areas of a LearningRx center targeting $720,000 a year in revenue:

Executive

How will we determine if we are creating an expanding, productive, and viable organization? Consider these three stats: gross revenues, net profit, and the profit percentage.

Gross revenues compared to the previous period tell us if we are growing and expanding. But they don't tell us if we're profitable or viable. *Net profit* is the difference between our revenues and expenses. It tells us if we made or lost money. But it doesn't tell us how well we ran our business.

What you need to look at is *profit percentage*. This is a measure of how much of your revenue ended up as profit (profit divided by revenues). When compared to industry standards and the amount invested in your business, it will give you an indication of how well you are running your company.

For our sample center (top of next page), here are the budgeted goals for the above stats. (I'm going to use "K" to represent $1,000 from here on. So $720,000 will be written as $720K.)

- Revenues $720K ($60K/month)
- Net Profit $144K ($12K/month)
- Profit Percentage 20% (profit/revenue—144K/720K)

Note that your profit percentage goal will likely be lower in your first few years of business. This is due to the facts that you'll probably invest greater sums into marketing at the outset, you'll have lower revenues at the beginning, and your fixed expenses will be a higher percentage of revenue.

Finances

How will you measure how well you are doing at collecting fees, paying bills, increasing cash flow, and reducing debt?

I would like to see you set your financial goals so that you collect *all* outstanding charges (no accounts receivable), pay *all* your bills when due (no accounts payable), reduce what you owe, and increase your savings. Sounds good, doesn't it?

Here's a principle to master: make sure your income is greater than your outgo. Make more than you spend. Spend less than you make.

Let's look at some sample numbers (top of the next page).

Accounts Payable refers to bills you haven't yet paid. You want this number to be zero at the end of every month. *Accounts Receivable* refers to charges that were made but not collected

- Accounts Payable (bills unpaid): $0
- Accounts Receivable (charges not collected) $120K
- Non-Controlled Receivables $0

for current deposit. These could include written agreements for credit card billings, post-dated checks to be deposited, or just the promise to pay in the next few months.

Non-Controlled Receivables would be charges for which you don't have the payments in hand. With these, you need to hope your customers keep their promise and send you the payments. This is not a good situation to be in. You want this number to be zero. You don't want to hope; you want those payments in your control.

My advice would be to collect all payments within the time period of the program.

Operations

To plan and oversee your operations, there are numerous measurements you could use. Here are some to consider: productivity per full-time staff, percent of staff objectives being met, ratio of income-producing staff to administrative staff, and revenue per square foot. Over time you may change what you measure as you find what best defines the pulse of your business.

Some sample numbers:

- Productivity/Staff hour $60/hr
- % of Objectives Met   75%
- Production hours: Administration hours   4:3
- Revenue/Square feet $600

When you're just starting out, don't use the measurements mentioned above. Instead, start by creating a budget that estimates your expense categories by percentage and then each month compare the actual costs to the budget and see where they are different. Then ask *why* they're different.

For example, after setting aside 20 percent as profit (see Chapter 12), for our example we'll divide the remaining 80 percent as follows:

- 10% ($72K/year)—royalties
- 12.5% ($90K/year)—marketing
- 7.5% ($54K/year)—facilities (rent, maintenance, etc.)
- 20% ($144K/year)—trainers
- 15% ($108K/year)—administrative staff
- 15% ($108K/year)—everything else

In Chapter 9, we'll look at some of these categories more closely when we discuss the dangers of not properly managing expenses.

Marketing

Here's where we take that $90K in our budget and think about how to use it to make our center better known among potential customers.

This is the one key area where measurements can make or break you. If you are clueless about which marketing efforts are working and which are not, you could be throwing big dollars away. If you don't have a thought-out plan, you're susceptible to every park bench, grocery cart, billboard, and cab sign sales pitch. You need good information to make smart choices. You need information like cost-per-prospect by marketing type, which marketing efforts are most effective, and which ones reach your ideal prospect the best.

With the revenue goals we've set and some additional information from past years, we can arrive at our marketing objectives. For example, to generate new revenue of $720K this year, with an estimated average case size of $5K, we'll need 144 new students this year. If we average 4 new students out of every 10 prospects, we'll need 360 prospects this year, or 30 per month. Our budgeted marketing investment is $90K, which allows us to invest up to $250 to create each prospect ($90K/360). You can see how these numbers need to be congruent to make sense.

- Marketing budget: $90K ($7.5K/mo)
- Number of prospects: 360 (30/mo)
- Cost per prospect: $250

Sales

You should have goals and stats for your sales function, too. To reach your annual revenue goal you'll need to know the number of new students needed each month and the average case size.

The case size refers to the amount customers pay for the LearningRx program they choose. In our example of a center with a $720K annual revenue goal, if the average case size is $5,000, you'll need to convert 144 prospects to students in one year—that's 12 a month.

We can measure our sales effectiveness by calculating our different conversion ratios. We can look at the percentage of prospects that become assessments and the percent of assessments that become students. And for an overall conversion rate, we can examine the percent of prospects that become students. Here are those ratios with needed goals for our example:

• Number of students:	144 (12/mo)
• Average Case Size:	$5K
• Prospects to Assessments:	80%
• Assessments to Students:	50%
• Prospects to Students:	40%

Products

Your monthly budget for the products category refers to the cognitive training services your trainers deliver to your students.

If the average fee per student is $5,000 and the average length of training is five months, then the average fee per student per month is $1,000. A quick way of determining how you are doing each month is to multiply the number of active students by $1,000. To average $60K per month you should have 60 active students.

• Number of Active Students:	60
• Average percentile gain in core skills:	30
• Average percentile gain in Word Attack:	25

To determine the effectiveness of your training, evaluate your pre- and post-test findings. You should see average percentile gains of weak skills of between 25 and 35.

Quality Control

In the LearningRx environment, your center gets multiple sources of feedback about the quality of your services. This happens first after the consultation, next when a mid-program call is made, and finally through the survey that customers take after their program review.

One of the key items on that survey is the question in which customers are asked to rank from zero to 10 how likely they are to refer their friends to LearningRx. Read Chapter 11 for a complete discussion of this very important measurement, called the Net Promoter Score (NPS).

Now You Know

Now you don't have to guess how well you're doing. With these

- Average score (0–10):   9 out of a possible score of 10
- Average NPS: 70 (see Chapter 11)

stats and measurements you can see what you are or are not achieving—and can now make good decisions on what needs your attention.

Key #4: Make Sure Every Function is Assigned To Someone

The fourth key to the success of your center is to be sure someone is personally responsible for progress in each of your core functions. Who is in charge of creating financial reports at your center? What about staff training? The facility itself? The referral system?

An activity that doesn't have someone accountable for seeing that it happens is an activity that will not get done.

Create a Key Area Board that you place in an employees-only spot in your center. Place the names or initials of your responsible parties on your Key Area Board. Arrange it so that at the top is the name of the person who has responsibility for all the names and activities under it, and a name under the top one has responsibility for those activities and people under it, and so forth. A graphical display like this will show everyone the chain and flow of responsibility in your center.

Here's an example for the key area of Operations:

OPERATIONS (pg)

Administration
    Admin Staff
    Staff Records
    Student Records (jc)
    Reception/Tel (jc)
    Manuals
    Forms

Trainers (kb)
    Hiring (kb/pg)
    Training
    Observation
    Scheduling

Facilities (jc)

Viewing the above you can see that **pg** has overall responsibility for Operations and all activities under it, unless assigned to someone else. The person whose initials are **jc** has responsibility for student records, reception and telephone, facilities. **jc** reports to **pg**. **kb** has responsibility for all functions under Trainers except hiring, which is shared with **pg**.

Conclusion

Our Japanese friends must have been mightily confused why Americans would want defective products in their order. But they went ahead and complied. If they could have done it in the way that seemed best to them, there would have been *zero* defects in what they provided.

You may not be able to provide flawless service to every one of your LearningRx customers, but it's a good goal to have! Your goals will determine where you are headed, and a regular analysis of those goals will show you if you're making progress toward them. Finally, having someone assigned to each goal will help you be sure good things are happening even when you're not the one personally doing them.

There are many more keys to success at a LearningRx franchise. We'll be discussing others in the chapters that follow. But you won't get anywhere with those other keys if you don't have these first four in place.

Know what the components of your business are and how well you're succeeding in each one.

CHAPTER 9

Profitability Keys 5–9:
Bottom Line Marketing And Sales Principles That Work

IN CHAPTER 8, we looked at the first four keys to profitability in your LearningRx center. In this chapter we'll look at five keys that relate to marketing and sales.

Here are the keys we'll talk about in this chapter each in turn:

- Seek a direct response from every marketing dollar you spend
- Control the cost of creating prospects
- Build referral networks
- Convert phone calls to assessments
- Be an advocate for your prospect

Key #5: Seek a Direct Response from Every Marketing Dollar You Spend

This advice is so crucial it could be a book in and of itself. Maybe one day it will be.

Every new business owner must understand that marketing is not an expense; it is an investment. It is part of the initial outlay you must afford, every bit as integral to your business launch as buying or renting the building, the equipment, and the franchise itself. As you're figuring your launch expenses, you'd better have marketing on the budget sheet right alongside office equipment and your business license.

When you are a new business, people don't know about you. This is even truer when it's not only the business that is new but the service itself, as is so often the case when a LearningRx center opens in a new city. People don't know you or even why they should know you. They haven't yet discovered how much they need you.

How will they find out how much they need you?

Through marketing, of course.

Marketing is simply the act of letting people know you're there and you're offering a product or service that will help them solve problems they're aware of. You're a solution-provider, and when they know you're there they'll seek you out.

But it won't happen without marketing. This means that your marketing costs, especially at the outset, will be much higher for you—up to twice as high—than if you were a known business with a known product. The chart below shows the marketing cost-per-prospect relationship (assuming that for a known name and product the cost-per-prospect is $100).

Cost-per-Prospect Comparison

$100 Known Product Known Business Name	**$125** Known Product Unknown Business Name
$150 Unknown Product Known Business Name	**$200** Unknown Product Unknown Business Name

Are you budgeting your marketing dollars accordingly?

Direct Response Marketing vs. Branding

You may have heard the term *branding* as it relates to the public's recognition of a company or product. Branding seeks to create awareness of a product in enough minds so that your potential prospects eventually will call you. Branding requires deep pockets and it may take years for an awareness campaign to show results.

You don't have the time or money to wait to see if your branding works.

Direct response marketing, on the other hand, asks your potential prospects to respond directly back to you. Usually this means asking the prospect to call, visit a Web site, or walk into your center.

"Visit the friendly City Bank on the corner of Maple and

Fifth," is an attempt at branding. But "Visit the friendly City Bank on the corner of Maple and Fifth and open a savings account this week and we'll add $25 to your account" is a direct response approach because it is asking for an action—a direct response. The first is promoting an image but the second is asking the listener to become a customer within a week.

Direct response marketing will get you the largest return-on-investment (ROI) because you are actually building your brand while you're making sales. Furthermore, the sales component creates accountability in direct response marketing that allows you to see which advertising placement is most effective.

When you're using direct response marketing you're not interested in how many people remember your ad or feel more inclined to buy. You want a response. Awareness is a byproduct.

There is, of course, nothing saying that you can't work a little branding into your direct response. And indeed you should. Good branding engenders trust in your business. A good tagline, graphic design, and logo also can make it instantly clear what your business does, allowing users to go directly to your message without having to decide if you're worth listening to.

Bottom line: Spend your marketing dollars in direct response. You'll know how well it is working, you'll get customers quicker, and it should more than cover its cost. And at the same time it will help build your brand.

A couple of years after our first center opened in Colorado Springs, one of our employees told us that she rarely met someone with school-aged children who hadn't heard of LearningRx. This should be one of the goals in your community.

The Role of Marketing in the Quest to Break Even and Prosper

Almost every business begins in a negative cash-flow situation. It has taken a sizable investment to be ready for opening day, and so far there has been no money flowing in to offset those costs.

The hope is that when your center opens people will begin coming in and signing up for LearningRx programs, and your journey toward break-even can begin. Beyond that goal you can even glimpse what it might be like to be in the black.

But you can't just open your doors and hope people will flock in. They have to know about you and want what you're offering. Thus the need for marketing.

Marketing is the steam engine that will pull your center to the peak called Mt. Break-Even and beyond. You can't cut marketing in your early days or you'll never get to your desired destination.

I can't emphasize this enough. Until you get to your break-even point you have to keep growing your revenues. Which means you have to keep shoveling coal into that marketing engine. You have to keep spending for marketing—and not just at a level that will maintain your current revenues, but at a level that will grow them.

This means you will continue to operate at a loss—not a profit—until your marketing efforts have grown enough revenues.

Let's say your new center makes $20K in monthly revenue. Also, let's say your variable expense is 40 percent of that total—$8K. (Variable costs include expenses tied to the number of students and revenue, like trainer pay, student kit cost, and royalty.) If your fixed expenses are $12K and marketing expenses are $4K, you are losing $4K per month. (Fixed expenses are costs you have even if you don't have students, like: rent, administrative staff, and insurance.)

Here are those numbers again:

Income:	$20K
Variable Expenses (40%)	- $8K
Fixed Expenses	- $12K
Marketing	- $4K
Profit/Loss	**- $4K [That's: 20K-(8K+12K+4K)]**

Nobody would want to be in this situation. If you find yourself there and you are already down to minimal staff and can't change your rent and other fixed expenses, the tendency will be to reduce marketing to stop more losses.

Big mistake. If you do that, your losses will increase! Less marketing will produce less revenue, which means less money to pay fixed expenses and therefore bigger losses.

Here's what is likely to happen if you cut marketing in half to try to save money—a greater loss (top of next page):

	Before	After reducing marketing
Income:	$20K	$10K
Variable Expenses (40%)	- $8K	- $4K
Fixed Expenses	- $12K	- $12K
Marketing	- $4K	- $2K
Profit/Loss	**- $4K**	**- $8K (a greater loss)**

What you need to do is spend *more* on marketing to make more revenues to pay for all your expenses to earn a profit. In our example, if your marketing expense was $4K and you increase it to $9K, and that $5K increase produced $25K extra revenue, your profit statement would look like this:

	Before	After
Revenues:	$20K	$45K
Variable Expenses (40%)	-$8K	-$18K
Fixed Expenses	-$12K	-$14K
Marketing	-$4K	-$9K
Profit/Loss:	**-$4K**	**$4K**

Here's the point: your marketing drives your revenue.

In studies of our centers in the last three years, the top third of our centers had revenues twice as high as those in the bottom third. The marketing cost to get a prospect was equal in both groups. That is, the bottom third could have had the same revenue as the top third if they had spent the same amount in marketing.

But they didn't—they spent only half on marketing and therefore got only half the revenue. But their profit wasn't half; it was a lot less than half because of a higher percentage of their revenue going to fixed expenses.

When Marketing is Not Cost-Effective

Not all marketing is created equal. If you choose marketing efforts that cause every marketing dollar to garner you two dollars in new revenue, you'll actually be falling deeper into the red.

For example, if you were to spend an additional $10,000 this month on marketing and it garnered you only an additional $20,000 in revenues, you would end up with an even larger loss than if you had not spent that money.

You need to be shooting for a much higher revenue gain per marketing dollar spent. If you spent that same $10,000 on marketing efforts that garnered you $80,000 in new revenue, you'd be doing well. Aim for marketing strategies that will generate at least $5 of revenue for every $1 of marketing money spent.

This number is often referred to as your marketing ROI (Return on Investment): the revenues earned for each marketing dollar spent. In our sample budget in the previous chapter, the expected ROI is 8 ($720K in revenues divided by $90K of marketing investment).

Finding the ROI Break-Even Point

There's a range of effectiveness in your marketing efforts. Fail to spend enough and your business will suffer, but increase your spending on ineffective marketing strategies and your business will likewise suffer.

How do you determine the minimal amount you need to spend and the minimal ROI your marketing needs to achieve?

I've developed two formulas to help you determine this. The first helps you find the minimal marketing ROI you'll need to break even. The second helps you determine the minimal amount you'll need to invest in marketing to hit that break-even point. They will require a little algebra, but I'll walk you through it.

In the following formulae I'll use some letters to stand for things. M stands for your minimum marketing investment. F stands for a non-marketing fixed expense. V is what percentage of revenue is your variable expense. And X is your ROI.

First, we'll look at how to find the minimum ROI you'll need to break even. You want to arrive at a situation in which X (ROI) is at least 5, though if you can get it to 10 you'll be doing great.

Here's the formula:

$$X=(F+M)/(1-V)M$$

If you were to read this in regular English you'd get something like this: Your X (ROI) is what you get when you add your fixed expenses to your marketing investment and then divide those things by your marketing investment times what's left of your revenues after you subtract your variable expenses.

So let's apply this to our example center. Remember, this center has fixed expenses of $12K/month, spends $4K/month on marketing, and has variable expenses of 40 percent of its monthly revenues.

$$X=(12+4)/(1-.4)4$$

See where those numbers came from? So now let's do the math.

$$12+4=16$$

$$1-.4=.6$$

$$\text{and}$$

$$.6*4=2.4$$

So now our formula looks like this:

$$X=16/2.4$$

And to finish out the math, we get an X (or ROI) of **6.67**. That's good. It's above 5. But it's below 10, so the center shouldn't be completely content.

That's how the center is doing now. But let's turn to finding what the center's minimal marketing spending should be to break even. For this we need a new formula:

$$M=F/(X-XV-1)$$

We're using the same variables. It's just that this time we know X (the ROI we want) and we're trying to find how much money we should spend on marketing to get to the break-even.

Read in English, this formula would say that to find what we should spend on marketing, we should take our fixed expense total and divide it by our ROI minus our ROI times our variable expenses, minus one.

So let's say our center has a marketing ROI of 5, and now we'll plug in the numbers:

$$M=12/(5-(5*.4)-1)$$

See where that came from? The center's fixed expenses are $12K/month, the current ROI from marketing is 5, and variable expenses are 40 percent (.4). Now let's do the math:

$$M=12/(5-2-1)$$

which is

$$M=12/2$$

which is

$$M=6$$

So our center must spend $6,000 per month on marketing to break even using the current marketing efforts. If you want to make a profit you will need to spend more than $6,000 and/or improve your ROI.

Why Not Spend More on Marketing?

I hope you can see that, even with your current marketing ROI, if you were to spend more on marketing you could go from a loss to a profit. With this kind of rational evidence, why don't struggling businesses spend more on marketing?

Here's what they say:

- "I never understood that marketing was an investment."

- "I don't have the extra money to do all that marketing."

- "I'm not sure where to spend my marketing money, so I don't spend it at all."

Following these excuses is a great way to drive your business to failure.

Maximized Marketing for Franchise Success

Let's look at a real case study. This franchise was on its way to collapse but began implementing these principles and has turned itself around.

Here are the stats we'll use for this case study:

- Marketing cost per prospect: $145

- Prospect-to-Assessment conversion rate: 43% (this is a very poor conversion rate, by the way)

- Average case or program size: $5,347

- Assessment-to-Student conversion rate: 42%

- Revenue (annual): $246K

- Marketing expenditures: -$36K

- Variable expenses: -$101K (41% of revenues)

- Fixed expenses: -$134K

- Profit/Loss: -$25K (loss)

This business was operating at a $25,000 loss for the year. Now, what will happen to this business if its leader doesn't spend more marketing dollars to increase revenue? One of these scenarios will play out:

- The owner will end up working for nothing—or, worse, will have to pay to work at his own business;

- The owner will use up his financial reserves until enough referrals kick in; or

- The most likely scenario is that the business will fail

within two years. The failure will come not because of the product, system, or marketing pieces, but because the owner wouldn't invest in marketing!

However, if this business were to double its investment in marketing and increase its prospect-to-assessment rate (by using a call center or replacing the receptionist), quite another outcome would result. See how easy it is to know what to do when you have the stats in front of you and take the time to analyze them?

Here are this business's expenses and earnings before and after doubling the amount it spent on marketing and fixing its prospect-to-assessment conversion rate:

	Before	After
Marketing cost per prospects:	$145	$145
Prospect-to-Assessment conversion rate:	43%	60%
Average case or program size:	$5,347	$5,347
Assessment-to-Student conversion rate:	42%	42%
Revenue (annual):	$246K	$492K
Marketing expenditures:	-$36K	-$72K
Variable expenses (41%):	-$101K	-$202K
Fixed expenses:	-$134K	-$174K
Profit/Loss	**-$25K (loss)**	**$44K (profit)**

That's a nearly $70K turnaround.

Your marketing spending is directly related to your income. It's as essential as buying the equipment you need or as hiring the personnel for your center. Without it, you might as well not even be open. In your first year, especially, marketing should be considered a capital investment. And as your center grows, marketing remains a key component in the health of your franchise.

You have heard that 80 percent of businesses fail within five years. Franchise businesses fare better than that, but still 20 percent of franchise businesses fail in the same time period. We're often told that by far the No. 1 reason for this failure is a shortage of capital.

I had a hard time believing that, because my experience was working with professional medical practices where that wasn't the case. But now that I've been working with small businesses for many years, I'm convinced it's true. Too many small businesses reduce the money spent on marketing before they have built their businesses big enough to properly cover their fixed expenses.

You need to keep spending on marketing and you need to keep testing your marketing to get the best possible return on your marketing investment.

Key #6: Control Prospect Costs

To be a sharp marketer means measuring and analyzing your results. You should know the number of people who responded and purchased from your different marketing efforts. With this information you will know the cost per prospect and cost per sale for each effort. This information, along with knowing your market and how best to reach it, is important in planning your next marketing steps.

Study the numbers below. Take it as a given that they are based on equal dollars spent with the same conversion rates and case size. As you look at these figures, consider what changes you would make for the coming year. Then compare your observations with mine to see if we are on the same page.

Here are the costs, by marketing category, for generating a single prospect. (These are our actual 2007 average costs/prospect by marketing category.):

• Radio Ad	$486
• Newspaper Ad	$349
• Direct Mail	$205
• TV Ad	$567
• Ad in Parenting Magazines	$171
• Referral	$9
• Internet Ad	$54

If all these marketing efforts penetrate your market equally well (i.e., if they reach the same families in the same numbers for the same effect) then I would just drop the ones that cost more. Why wouldn't you go with the marketing solutions that cost less per referral?

However, as I said before, not all marketing is created equal. No single marketing effort reaches your entire market. This means you need to use multiple types of marketing.

What efforts would you use, given these numbers?

No matter what, I would keep pushing for increased referrals. That's always the best and cheapest means of marketing.

But referrals might get you only 20 percent of the students you need. I would also greatly expand the Internet efforts because those are pretty cheap. However, as of 2007, about 50 percent of your market doesn't use the Web yet.

I would consider dropping my TV ads, but might first try some better-targeted channels or perhaps present a different message or make a different offer with a greatly reduced ad budget. I would reduce the total dollars spent on radio and newspaper ads and would increase direct mail and parenting magazine ads.

When you know how much marketing money you have to spend to generate a prospect you can begin making strategic decisions about how to spend that marketing money. Without these numbers you won't have any real idea how to modify your marketing. That is why you need measurable objectives and goals.

Key #7: Build Referral Networks

This is the way to go. Referred prospects are your bread and butter. They're more likely to become students, they're often already sold on LearningRx, they tend to have higher case sizes, and the cost per prospect is very low.

To get a referred prospect you must have certain things going. You must have current students, of course, because they'll be doing the referring. And to get customers you will need to buy them with marketing dollars (refer to Key #6). You have to *wow* your current customers so they want to refer (more on that in Chapter 11). You need to ask your current customers to refer, or they may just not think to do it. And you need some kind of a rewards system so the referrals aren't hit and miss.

Thousands of pages of books and articles have been written about getting referrals. Everyone knows it's the best way to grow your business, but it's often poorly done. It's not easy to get consumers to refer. What's in it for them? They have a lot to lose if they refer someone to you and you blow it. Nor is it easy for them to bring up the fact that their child has (or had) learning or reading problems. Given the no-win nature of most referrals, here are three ideas to consider:

- First, referrals will happen more often if the consumer can give something of value and low risk to their friends—like a coupon for a high-value, low-cost assessment or a free book.

- Second, your center needs to be worthy of a referral. Wow your students and their parents and they'll tell others about you.

- Third, train all your staff to refer to people they encounter in their lives outside of LearningRx. They need to share those 'wow' experiences they have been part of.

Key #8: Convert Calls to Assessments

Answer the phone.

You'd think that would be a no-brainer, but at businesses across the nation millions of incoming calls go unanswered—and millions of dollars of revenue are lost.

In a recent study of health care centers, only 21 percent of calls that came in during normal weekday office hours were answered.

Twenty-nine percent weren't answered within eight rings and the callers finally hung up. Fifty percent went to the answering machine—but only 45 percent of those callers left a message. And less than 15 percent left messages asking to schedule an appointment.

If the phone in your center doesn't get answered you will lose a large percent of that potential business.

You need either a full-time receptionist or a call center. Every call answered by a call center will cost you an average of $10—and roughly 40 percent of those calls could turn into $5,000 cases. As we've seen, you're already spending $150 to $250 in marketing money to generate a single prospect. Why not spend another $10 to convert those prospects to customers?

While one of our support staff was visiting a new center she noticed that the phone was not being answered. She challenged the director to answer every call in the next hour. The result: four scheduled appointments!

Every 10 unanswered calls represent four lost customers. So by letting these 10 calls go unanswered you're saving $100 dollars (by not having a receptionist or call center) but you're losing $20,000. It's like throwing away $200 to save $1.

Key #9: Be the Prospect's Advocate

I'll confess, back in 1986 my prospect-to-student conversion rate was 11 percent for my first 75 consultations (those were all done on one Saturday—also not terribly smart). Over the next few years I improved my process until my conversion rate reached 50 percent.

But the biggest single jump (from 50 percent to 70 percent) took place when I wasn't doing consultations for myself but for Tanya's business. The reason: I wasn't concerned about my well-being. I wasn't focused on making a sale (especially since Tanya wasn't paying me anything). Instead, I was concerned about making sure the student got the help he or she needed.

If you want to convert prospects to customers, you need to get in their corner.

It sounds like a small point but it has large ramifications. When you are an advocate for people who are struggling, your needs will be met in meeting theirs.

If you want to convert prospects to customers, you need to get in their corner.

The secret to success in LearningRx sales is empathizing with your prospects' pain and listening to their concerns. These people are hurting. They're troubled. Someone in his or her family—maybe even the prospect herself—is struggling to succeed. This has left them feeling embarrassed and frustrated and alarmed about the future.

And yet they've called you. They've heard about you and they have some sliver of hope that you can help them.

Don't rush into the sales pitch. Take a minute just to empathize. You got into this business because you wanted to help people, right? If you just wanted to make a profit you could've bought some other kind of franchise. But you care about the hurts of people in your community and you want to bring them the means to get help.

So just listen. Listen with concern and love and compassion.

How many times have you had someone do that for you and afterward you felt encouraged, and were willing to buy into just about whatever they were selling? I'm not saying you should be hypocritical and only pretend to care; I'm saying that your genuine concern will have a positive effect when it comes time for these prospects to think about signing up for a LearningRx program.

A good way to learn to listen is to ask questions. In fact, your consultation should be a series of questions with you listening and leading the customer to the answer they are seeking by each next question you ask. The consultation is made up of four big questions:

FOUR BIG QUESTIONS:

1. What is your situation?

2. What are the problems?

3. How do the problems impact your family?

4. How do you see our solution helping you?

I've always had the dream of doing an entire consultation with no statements, only questions. You may not be able to achieve that, but it should be your concentration as you conduct the consultation. You ask, then you listen.

Questions are so important. They are your diagnostic tools to help you figure out what's behind the words you're hearing. They help you uncover answers.

Once, after returning from a trip, my neighbor told to me that my son Brett had been on our roof shooting pellets at my neighbor's "House for Sale" sign. When Brett returned from school I told him that I was aware he had done something wrong while I'd been gone. "Why don't you tell me about what you did?" I said.

Brett proceeded to launch into a whole list of misdeeds he'd done while I'd been gone – apparently he'd been a busy boy! Most of his transgressions involved a non-approved party he'd had at our home. Finally he named the one offense I did know about. Questions uncover all kinds of problems you might otherwise never know about.

Another time I was talking with my closest friend's daughter about her relationship with her fiancé. They were soon to be married but I had a few concerns. So I asked questions. Her answers revealed some pain, which led to further questions. I don't recall that I did anything but ask questions during that entire 90-minute conversation. But at the end of it she had determined that this pending marriage wasn't right and she was willing to accept whatever criticism would come from canceling a wedding within a month of the wedding date. By the way, she and her parents still thank me. Questions reveal consequences. Questions lead to actions.

If you combine your questions with authentic empathy and a conviction that the value of your programs is worth far more than your fees, you'll regularly convert prospects to customers.

Forget your needs of income and minimize the parents' concern about costs. Concentrate on representing the students and make sure they get what is needed to make their life far better. And if what we offer doesn't match their need, send them somewhere else. That is your role in the consultation.

Conclusion

The interface between the community and your center is marketing and sales. This is the phase that takes strangers unaware of your services and converts them to thrilled customers raving to their friends about your center. Without this—the front door, so to speak—people won't come in and get to know you. But with proper marketing and sales approaches, the community will beat a path to your center.

The keys are to seek a direct response from every marketing dollar you spend, to control your prospect costs, to build referral networks, to answer the phone, and to be your prospect's advocate.

Do these well and you may find yourself among the top LearningRx franchises in the country, too.

CHAPTER 10

Profitability Keys 10–13:

Policies that Remove Stress

RUNNING A BUSINESS is stressful, especially at the beginning. In this chapter, I'll outline four best-practice policies that, if followed, will remove much of that stress.

Key #10: Collect Your Fees

We're going to delve into customer psychology here for a minute. Did you know that a customer who is required to pay the entire owed amount up front is 1) more likely to pay it all and 2) more likely to be a satisfied customer than someone who is paying it off over time?

Think about it: If all a customer's services have been rendered before payment is due, he will have no urgency to pay you at all. "Hey, I'm not in pain now; there is no rush to pay for this right away."

Once services have been rendered, it hurts to pay. The

customer will begin looking for ways to get out of it. When the first invoice comes in, he may say, "Was it really worth it?" When the second invoice comes in, he may say, "No, it wasn't worth it." And when the third invoice comes in, he may say, "It was a rip-off! No way am I paying!" And then you're in trouble. You may end up not only without full payment but with an upset and negative client.

It's going to sound strange but you'll do your customer a favor if you collect all your fees up front.

Here are three ways of collecting your fees early on:

- First, give your customers a discount on their total bill when they pay it all up front. This helps them with the bottom line and brings the money into your hands fully and early.

- Second, make financing (i.e., educational loans) available to your customers. The loan company will pay you everything up front and it will be the customer's job to pay the company—and the company's job to make sure the customer pays.

- Third, sometimes your customer may want to set up a payment plan with you, not a financing company. If so, then collect as much as possible up front and handle the balance with either a post-dated check or a written agreement that authorizes you to charge their credit card for a set amount over the next few months.

Whatever you set up, keep in mind the goal of getting the money early in the process, while the customer is still receiving services. It keeps you in the black and it actually helps raise your customer's satisfaction level with your services.

Tip: Using post-dated checks is a wonderful process for many situations. I first used it 40 years ago with a tenant who was always paying late. Since then it's become our standard policy for family loans, rentals, or anything in which future payments are involved. Make life easier: collect the money up front.

Key #11: Pay Your Bills When They Are Due

A wise man once wrote, "Owe nothing to anyone except to love one another."

When it comes to bills in business you would do well to owe no man anything. Pay all your bills when they're due. Keep the amount you owe (your accounts payable, or A/P) at zero every month.

We're talking about your reputation as a business and a businessperson. Keep it good. Other people don't have any reason to keep quiet about your inability—or simple failure—to pay your bills. In fact, they'll love to tell as many others as possible that you don't pay your bills. This is because your failure to pay has made them angry and they are getting even with you.

If you're operating within your budget, then paying your bills in full and on time should be no problem. Your comfort, your peace of mind, and your ability to get a good night's sleep require it. This pillar of business excellence is one of the easiest to achieve. All you have to do is write out the checks.

As for your method of accounting, I recommend you use the cash system. I know that may make your accountant scream but unless you're a large company, using the cash method is the easiest and the most sensible.

When a bill comes in, put it in a folder on the desk. Don't enter it into the computer yet. Then, twice a month (such as the 5th and the 20th) open that folder and enter those bills into your accounting software. Make it one process: bill gets entered; check gets printed; envelope gets stuffed, stamped, and delivered.

Make life easier: collect the money up front.

This system works great, providing that you're paying all bills when they're due.

Key #12: Control Your Fixed Expenses

Your fixed expenses are things you must pay for every month even if you have no students. They include rent, administrative salaries, insurance, telephone, and utilities. (Marketing is not a normal expense, as I say elsewhere in this book—it is an investment.) Strive to keep your fixed expenses low.

Let's look at the rent you pay for your facility. You've heard the adage that success in business is about three things: location, location, location. Well, that's certainly true for restaurants and retail stores but it's not as vital for service businesses like LearningRx. You want to be visible and conveniently located, of course, but you don't have to pay lots of extra money to nab the most high-visibility corner of First and Main.

If you choose a facility that costs you $8,000 per month over one that will cost you $4,000 per month, keep in mind that you'll have to generate an additional $40,000 per month in revenue if you've budgeted rent at 10 percent of your total expenses!

A 1,200-square-foot training space with 10 training stations used for four hours a day, six days a week, can produce more than $1 million per year. You don't need a cavernous warehouse for training.

And while we're talking about space, don't make the biggest room in your center your office. Wait until you have four or five successful centers—of course, by then you won't need the ego boost a large office gives. Wouldn't you rather have a smaller office and more (money-making) training space?

One way to keep your fixed expenses under control is to not assume they're really fixed. Sometimes you can get those "fixed" expenses lowered, which will have an immediate positive effect on your bottom line. It is my belief that you can negotiate almost anything. Here's a story from Tanya:

> I watched my dad negotiate almost everything. Just recently he was able to negotiate a two-for-one manager's special when there wasn't one. It was a chain shoe store. He even got shoelaces and polish thrown in!
>
> Most times all he does is ask. But sometimes he uses other tactics. One time he made an offer on a used car. The seller wasn't going for it. So Dad had our whole family get into our old car and he informed the salesman that his offer was good until he couldn't see the salesman in the rear-view mirror. He got in and we drove away. We were about a block away when the salesman ran into the street waving to indicate that he had accepted Dad's offer.

Dad is frugal when it comes to most things and gets tremendous deals, but seldom at the expense of people. This is displayed by the large tips he often leaves for salespeople and waiters—not always because of good service but because he feels they need to be blessed.

Key #13: Control Your Administrative Expenses by Making Them Variable

It is said that the definition of insanity is doing the same thing over and over and hoping for different results. That kind of craziness can definitely result when it comes to hiring administrative staff for your LearningRx center.

When you start your franchise, the entire administrative staff may consist of you and one other person. You may not even be able to pay yourself a fair rate. It's OK to do that for awhile, but you can't keep it up forever. Slowly increase your own pay as your revenues increase until you reach the point where your pay equals what you would have to pay someone else to do your job. The fair market rate, in other words.

Then, after more growth, you can begin thinking about bringing on more administrative staff at a fair rate of pay.

But you have to be careful here because administrative expenses can become a cancer on your business. This one line item has the tendency to grow faster than any other expense category and to eat up more of your profits. And if you've got inefficient operating procedures in your center, you can end up hiring people and then not using them efficiently—resulting in the need to hire more people and throw away more profits.

Stop the madness!

Twenty years ago I faced this problem. My staff cost had increased to 28 percent compared to the normal 18 percent. I was hiring more people rather than increasing efficiency. That solution was easier but more expensive.

I solved the situation by making my staff "partners," promising that 20 percent of every dollar earned would go to them. Now they had a stake in the practice. In six months base salaries had dropped to 15 percent and income, productivity, and bonuses had become much higher. When considering another staff position, we would all determine if that position was really needed or whether could we figure out how to accomplish more with our current staff (fewer hands sharing the pot).

I now had control of staff costs. I had done so by making it no longer fixed but varied. Staff costs now went up or down, like my income, with the revenues.

Keep your administrative staff expenses in the range of one-half to two-thirds of what you're paying for trainers. Start with minimal administrative staff and go up only as your income goes up. If you keep this same percentage but increase your revenues, you'll increase the money you'll have available for administrative expenses and yet still be well within your budget.

If you hire another full-time administrator and it moves you out of the correct trainer-to-administrator ratio, start the new staff member as a trainer with just a few hours as administrator. Then, as revenues increase, reduce the person's training hours and increase administrative hours.

Growth is a beautiful thing in business. As revenues increase, your fixed expenses become a smaller and smaller percentage of your monthly totals, thus leaving room for more things you want to do—and more profits. When you see this happening, you know you're managing well.

Conclusion

Business in today's economy can be maddening. And no one feels the burden and anxiety more than you, the franchisee.

But you can minimize your stress by collecting your fees, paying your bills on time, keeping your fixed costs low, and putting your administrative expenses in their proper percentage range.

Do these things and not only will your stress drop, your profitability will increase.

CHAPTER 11

Profitability Key 14:

The Wow Factor

WE HAD JUST MOVED to Colorado Springs and I had opened a checking account at 1stBank. It was a small bank branch inside the closest gas station. A few weeks later as I walked into the branch, Angie, the teller who had set up my account, greeted me by name. She inquired about my wife and mother, also by name.

I was impressed. I had never encountered a business so friendly. I loved them since they treated me as if I were their only customer, and so I told others about them. Today there are at least 27 accounts at that bank as a result of my word of mouth. Why would anyone bank anywhere else?

1stBank wowed me, and great things followed. So it must be for your LearningRx franchise. Indeed, wowing is so vital to the well-being of your center that I've given it its own chapter.

In order for your franchise to succeed over the long haul, you need satisfied customers out there telling other people what a great service you provide. Customers do this when they have not only gotten what they expected out of their interactions with your center, but when they have gotten *more* than they expected. When they have been wowed.

Expectations Plus

When someone agrees to purchase a LearningRx program she is not yet a satisfied customer. She's not yet loyal to your center or to you. You have earned the chance to prove yourself, and that's all. In fact, she's going to feel like she's just done you a big favor and that you owe her now.

In the sense of customer satisfaction, you start your relationship in a position of deficit. The customer has paid. Now it's your turn to produce.

And don't think that simply providing the service she expects will result in a satisfied customer at the end of the program. If she expects X and you deliver X, you'll still be at a zero at the end of your time together. At that point you wouldn't owe her. You'd no longer be at a deficit in her eyes. But neither would she owe you anything—such as going out and telling everyone to come enroll in your program.

High customer satisfaction results from whatever positives you give beyond X. It's when your customer expected X and you provided X+5 that she becomes motivated to tell others about your center.

That extra beyond her expectations is what I call the *"wow factor."* You want people out there saying, "I expected LearningRx to help my child, but I had no idea they'd do *this* for me."

That's a wowed customer.

The Net Promoter Score (NPS)

Fred Reichheld is considered America's leading expert in customer loyalty. Reichheld, who teaches at the Harvard Business School, wrote an influential book called *The Ultimate Question: Driving Good Profits and True Growth* (Harvard Business Press, 2006). In it, he develops a simple test to determine whether your customer has been wowed.

Reichheld boils it down to one ultimate question (which I've adapted for LearningRx):

> *On a scale of 0 to 10, how likely is it that you would recommend this LearningRx center to a friend or colleague?*

The customer takes a short survey at the end of the student's program. This question is only one of the items in that survey but it is the most important piece of data we collect.

In Reichheld's system, customers who answer 9 or 10 on this question are considered *Promoters*. They will go out and tell people how wonderful you, your center, and LearningRx are. They will act like volunteer marketing reps for your center.

On the other extreme are customers who answer 0 through 6. These are considered *Detractors*. They will go out and tell everyone their horror stories about working with you. In our day, when a single blog entry can reach tens of thousands of potential clients, you can't afford to have many Detractors out there.

Customers who answer this question with a 7 or 8 are considered neutral and are not included in the calculations to follow.

Hopefully you will have many more people answering 9 or 10 on this survey than those answering 6 or lower. But it's inevitable that you'll have both. You want to make sure you have the most Promoters and the fewest Detractors as possible.

Reichheld takes the percentage of Promoters and subtracts from that the percentage of Detractors (ignoring the percentage of neutrals) to arrive at any business' Net Promoter Score (NPS).

So if you had 100 customers and 50 of them gave you a score of 9 or 10, that's considered a Promoter score of 50 percent. And then let's say that 30 of them gave you a score of 0 to 6. Your Detractor score is 30 percent. To find your NPS you simply subtract the Detractor score from the Promoter score. In this case, it would be 50-30, giving you a NPS of 20.

An NPS of 20 is not bad—especially considering that the average business in the United States scores an NPS between nine and 11—but it's not nearly high enough for your center to thrive as you're wanting it to.

Here are recent NPS scores from the leaders in a number of industries in the U.S.

Industry		Winners: Highest Promoter
Airlines	60	Southwest
Rental Car	53	Enterprise
Car Brands	74	Saturn
Full Service Brokerage	64	AG Edwards
Retail Banks	66	Commerce Bank
Cell Phones	42	SBC
Health Insurance	47	AFLAC
Life Insurance	72	USAA
Shipping/Delivery	66	FedEx
Department Stores	59	Target
Drug Stores	55	Walgreens

You can see that an NPS of 20 isn't going to exactly make you an industry leader. You've got to shoot much higher.

It's good, then, that you've joined the LearningRx family. Across the system our franchisees give the home office an NPS that has never been below 68—and our center customers have never rated our programs below 70! So you've got a good system helping your business provide customers with that wow factor.

Raising Your NPS

Reichheld's system is as helpful as it is simple. Just increase the number of Promoters and decrease the number of Detractors and your NPS is going to rise. Studies show that for every 12 percentage points your NPS rises, your annual growth rate will double.

So how do you raise your NPS? By increasing the wow factor. Here's how:

Create a Positive High-Energy Atmosphere in Your Center

In terms of improving customer satisfaction, it is essential that your trainers and staff fully own the solutions. One way to get this is to have your staff involved in brainstorming ideas of how better to wow parents and students.

Author Ken Blanchard tells the story of such a brainstorming session at a supermarket, when a young man named Johnny—a 19-year-old grocery bagger with Down syndrome—came up with an idea that's now reported on thousands of Web sites and retold in many customer-service books.

> *"Every night after work, I'd come home and find a thought for the day [on the Internet]. If I can't find a saying I like," he added, "I just think one up!" He printed them from his computer, cut out each quote, and signed his name on the back. Then he'd put the thought for the day in the customer's bag.*
>
> *Within weeks his checkout line became three times longer than anyone else's. When the manager saw that, he called for another line to open and tried to get people to change lines. But no one would move. They said, "No, it's OK—we want to be in Johnny's lane—we want his 'Thought for the Day.'"*

Great service comes from the heart.

Will you be a Johnny?

Reward Trainers for Turning Customers into Promoters

Ninety percent of your customer's contact with LearningRx will be through that one trainer the student is assigned to. More than the programs, the facilities, or anything that happens in the reception room, a customer's satisfaction will be measured in terms of how that trainer did with that student.

Doesn't it make sense, then, that a trainer who consistently turns customers into Promoters be recognized and rewarded for that? If that trainer's excellence boosts your NPS, shouldn't you acknowledge and value that?

By the same token, if a trainer consistently turns customers into Detractors, that needs to be taken into account as well.

That's precisely what Fred Reichheld believes, and I think any center that desires to grow and be great would be wise to listen to him. In other words, build in your trainers an ownership for customer satisfaction by making promotions, bonuses, and firing decisions based on overall customer satisfaction.

Make trainers accountable for the results of the ultimate question of "Would you refer a friend or colleague to LearningRx?"

Customers become Promoters only when they believe they are receiving a high-quality program where all the core value aspects are being covered; where staff and trainers are loving and caring; and where price, value, and quality are all appropriate.

So make your trainers accountable for the satisfaction of every customer in their care. Reward your trainers when those customers turn into Promoters. And watch your NPS scores rise.

Become an Exemplary LearningRx Leader

Customer service is not the job of your marketing person—it's your job. The responsibility for excellent customer satisfaction begins and ends with you. Your NPS scores will rise as you ensure that you're providing a positive customer experience. You do this in a number of ways.

First, set the example. Be your center's benchmark for exemplary customer service. Your staff will pick up on your responsiveness to customer concerns and they'll follow your lead. Customers and staff alike will see that your key goal is meeting the needs of your customers and students.

In formulating your personal values in business, make sure that *effective service* is near or at the top of your list. It flows from the Second Great Commandment (to love others) and the Golden Rule (to treat others as you want to be treated). Because just as a commitment to excellent customer care is contagious, so is unresponsiveness to customer concerns. Treat your customers not only as you would want to be treated, but as you want your staff to treat customers.

Second, make customers feel welcome. This happens in two major phases: the initial consultation and the daily routine. There are few things as powerful as first impressions, so make sure you're doing a great job with those initial interactions with potential customers.

Then be sure you're doing a good job with the little things your customer will encounter on a more daily basis. How often do you circulate through the center, stopping to chat with parents or play with kids? How many rings does it take before the phone is answered? How long does it take a caller to navigate through the phone system? Do you have a direct line where customers can reach you immediately if you're available?

A customer who feels welcomed in your center—and by you personally—is more likely to become a Promoter.

Great service comes from the heart.

Third, work the wow factor. What are the extras you can provide that will amaze your customers? What can you do that is above and beyond the call of duty? Often these extras will cost you nothing—remember Johnny?

When you consistently and creatively find ways to delight your customers and students, when you extravagantly exceed customers' expectations, when you under-promise and over-deliver, that's when you'll have customers who say, "I never imagined LearningRx would do *that* for me! I've got to tell my friends about this place."

I know of a student who has cerebral palsy. His brother, who also has cerebral palsy, is much higher functioning and had previously been through the LearningRx program with amazing gains. The parents were so impressed that they wanted their second son to receive the training as well.

The director was very frank in lowering expectations for the second son because his abilities were so low. Even so, the parents didn't hesitate. When he finished the program they reported that the benefits their son gained were far above anything they had ever done. "Before, he would just watch his brother and sisters play games—now he asks to play and be a part of the family."

What an unexpected gift LearningRx gave that family!

As the leader of your LearningRx center, you are uniquely positioned to overwhelm your customers with positive experiences. No one can do more than you to wow your customers.

Salvage Detractors

The final thing you can do to raise your NPS scores is to salvage Detractors. It's true that your customers will more readily remember the negative experiences they had at your center than the positive ones. They're only human, after all. If you are starting in a position of deficit with your customer and anything happens that increases that deficit, it will take longer to overcome that.

And sometimes you simply won't overcome it. It's unavoidable that some people will end up with a negative opinion about your center or the LearningRx programs. That may be because of unrealistic expectations at the beginning, because of something negative that happens along the way, or through simple miscommunication. 70 to 80 percent of all customer problems result from miscommunication.

The good news is that you can correct customers' false expectations, you can manage their expectations going forward, and you can reach out to Detractors and, in many cases, turn them into Promoters. Or if not Promoters, then at least non-hostiles.

It starts by managing expectations at the initial consultation. Don't allow your customers to believe that LearningRx is going to correct things that are probably beyond the reach of what it can do. Don't over-promise.

It continues when you promote your center's successes in public ways. Make sure your customers know the good things that are happening with your center and their students. Be on the alert constantly for the good things that your constituents should know about. Put your success stories in your newsletters, on tables in the reception area, and on walls. Use your public events to congratulate those who deserve it. If in doubt, publicize it!

Despite these efforts, you'll likely end up with Detractors—people who finish your program still considering that you are in a position of deficit to them. In their eyes you promised but didn't deliver, and they're going to make sure no one else gets burned like they were.

I vividly recall a woman who came back to my practice loudly demanding a refund on a pair of glasses she thought was wrong but I believed was not. Rather than negotiate with her I asked her how I could solve the problem. After I did what she wanted she said, "Thanks, I would now like to schedule my two other children." Someone who could've become a Detractor remained a loyal customer.

You need to reach out to these people. It is imperative that you salvage these relationships whenever possible. So pick up the phone and reopen those lines of communication.

For these and other conflicts with customers, use the following techniques:

Successful Conflict Resolution

To you, a customer problem seems like one more item on your to-do list. But to your customer, it is a crisis. Conflict must be addressed as quickly as possible—even immediately.

Sometimes you or someone at your center is the cause of the conflict. At other times it's the case of a customer being unreasonable. There are things you can do to successfully manage conflict in either case.

Approach the conflict in a professional, non-confrontational way, full of empathy. Consider the last time you received a traffic ticket. Think about how the police officer treated you. Policemen are trained to keep such exchanges quiet, non-confrontational, and very professional. That should be your approach, too—but with more empathy than the policeman probably had!

No matter whose fault the problem is, be sure you do these things as you attempt to resolve the conflict:

- Make only those promises you are sure you can keep.

- Take excellent notes of the conversation, and keep them in a file.

- Be pleasant.

- Keep your cool.

- Thank the customer for bringing the concern directly to you (or for being willing to discuss it, if you've made the initial contact).

To raise your NPS you need to keep those Detractors off the streets—or the information superhighway. Decrease the number of Detractors and your Promoters will be the only ones out there talking about your center.

Conclusion

Just as an unsatisfied customer can quickly spread a bad report across the Internet, so can an enthusiastic Promoter broadcast your excellence far and wide. Every customer who gives you a 9 or 10 in that satisfaction survey is an unofficial member of your marketing department. These people are out shouting your praises to anyone who might have a need that LearningRx could satisfy.

A horde of Promoters helps you in innumerable ways. Just on a practical level, think of how much marketing money it costs you to create a prospect and how much it takes to turn a prospect into a customer. Every additional Promoter you have out there multiplies the impact of your marketing, thus reducing your costs and increasing your revenues.

People will learn about LearningRx through advertising or fliers or events you hold or participate in. But no promotional activity carries more weight than wowed customers telling others about how wonderfully they were treated at your center.

Up the wow factor at your center and watch your franchise grow.

CHAPTER 12

Profitability Key 15:

Budget a Profit

TAKE OUT YOUR budget sheet. Go ahead and fire up the computer and load up the spreadsheet. Now, look at your list of expenses. Is "Profit" listed as one of your expenses?

That's right, I'm asking if you have *profit* listed as an expense. Do you?

The final key to profitability I want to give you is that you should consider profit as one more variable expense, and budget accordingly.

Most people think profit is whatever's left after everything else has been paid for. I'm here to tell you that there is a far wiser way to assure profit. Far better to sock away 15 to 25 percent of your monthly sales as a profit payment to yourself. Subtract it from your revenues and stick it in a savings account.

A Secret that Works

All my adult life I have used this principle in some form or another. And believe me, it works.

When you take out a percentage for profit just like any other bill to be paid, you'll learn to live on what's left. You'll budget within your means—and you'll have a built-in profit at the end of the month.

As I said earlier, we have a built-in tendency to spend all we have. If it's in the checking account, it can be spent. But when you put part of it in savings before you think about new spending, you'll have a profit.

In my first year out of graduate school I began putting 10 percent of all my earnings into investments. And if I made any money on those investments, 100 percent of that went right back into investments. For many years it meant cutting here and there to make it work. And to make it work, I had to establish personal spending policies that have now become fixed—such as always buying a 3to7-year-old car or, if the price of a drink at a restaurant is more than $1.50, ordering water. Putting 10 percent aside for savings is a practice that has served me well.

Joseph helped a Pharaoh save a nation using this same principle. During seven years of plenty, a portion of crops was put aside in a storehouse. When hard times came later, that reserve saved the nation.

As I write this, it's early November 2008—the country is going through its greatest financial downturn since the Great Depression of 1929. The stock market has dropped almost by half, there are more home foreclosures than ever before, there's talk about General Motors failing, and businesses are closing on every block.

The day I wrote this, I had a call from a franchisee sharing how tough things have been the past few months and wondering if she will be able to make it. If she had followed this advice and placed a percent of her revenue aside during the good times, that call would not have been made.

Budgeting a Profit in the LearningRx Context

Let's look at how you can do this with your center.

As I mentioned at the beginning of this chapter, your goal should be to put away 15 to 25 percent of your monthly revenue into savings as profit. However, when you are just launching your franchise you may have to make that a lower percentage. But don't go below 5 percent.

As your center matures and revenues go up, your fixed expenses will be a smaller percentage of your total budget and you can begin allocating more for that "expense" called profit.

Here's an example of what a break-even budget would look like if you were to build in a 15 percent profit as a variable expense:

- Variable Costs (49% of sales)

  Trainer salaries—19.5%

  Kit costs—2%

  Royalty—10%

  Marketing Development Fund—2.5%

  Profit—15%

- Fixed Costs (Total of $20,000/month)

    Administrator salaries—$6,000

    Rent—$3,500

    Marketing—$8,500

    Other—$2,000

If these are your costs, then the break-even formula would look like this:

- Subtract 49 cents of every dollar of sales to pay variable expenses (49%)

- That leaves 51 cents of every dollar of sales to pay fixed expenses (51%)

- To break even with these numbers, your center would need to make $39,216 in sales every month (that's the amount you'd need to make to pay $20,000 in fixed costs and have that $20,000 be just 51% of your budget)

- If your center's average fee per student is $5,000, then to generate $39,216 a month in revenue you'd need to add eight new students every month.

    Because 39,216/5,000 = 7.8 (rounded up to 8 students)

Just eight new students a month. That's not too much to ask for, is it? And that's with a 15 percent profit built in!

Conclusion

You can do this. It's much easier to put away 15 to 25 percent of your revenues for an expense than hope for profit. It also helps you psychologically if you do it this way, because you'll feel more like you're meeting your obligations (paying your bills) than splurging on yourself.

I've built a profit into every business I've owned. Yes, even your royalty fee. Ten percent of that gets socked away as profit.

That 10 percent has been a blessing not only for us but also many others. It has allowed us to grow, enjoy, and help others in ways that simply would not have been possible otherwise.

Profit is good. Make a profit with your center. What you do with that profit is the subject of chapter 14.

CHAPTER 13

Seven Mistakes To Avoid
(That Almost All New Business Owners Make)

FEELING EQUIPPED? Ready to get out there and apply all 15 of these keys and watch your franchise soar? Congratulations! I know you'll do well with an attitude like that.

As a final word on profitability, I want to help you step through a minefield. Starting a business is a tricky path but it's one that millions of people have been down before. You can learn from the mishaps of others and, hopefully, avoid most of these pitfalls yourself.

Don't worry if you've already committed one or more of these mistakes. Every business owner takes the occasional bad step. Making mistakes is how we learn and grow, after all.

But let's see if I can't help you step over some of these mines. Here are the seven mistakes that almost all new business owners make...

#1 New Business Mistake To Avoid—Thinking Too Big or Too Small

It's almost impossible to make a perfectly accurate guess about what's going to happen when you officially open the doors of your business. You do all you can, market to the best of your ability, prepare and polish and pray, but in the end, whatever's going to happen on Day one is going to happen.

That's just your starting place, of course, but whatever happens on that day can be a shock to you if you've anticipated too high or too low.

If you've been thinking too small, you may lose a potential opportunity. Perhaps you could've taken your business to a higher plateau from the very outset but you failed to do so because you didn't think such a thing was within your reach. Maybe you didn't feel confident in your launch because you were going up against a well-established competitor. Maybe you thought your marketing efforts had fallen on deaf ears. Whatever the cause, if you think too small you may not detect the opportunities to go big.

On the other hand, if you've been thinking too big, you may get yourself in a bind. You may over-commit yourself or go further into debt because you expected a certain response but reality shows that you grossly overestimated.

You need to remember that your center can handle only so much business at launch. You'll be able to support expansion later, but moving beyond your core business too soon can be like chasing 10 rabbits at once and catching none.

Be careful about expanding to a second location too soon.

You may think you've got this thing figured out because of the lessons you learned managing the first center, but a new location will require the same amount of capital as the first one. It also will take a whole new set of skills to manage a location that won't have your presence there full time, not to mention that you'll need to hire a trained staff that is capable of running a second location without you. Expanding without these things in place will very likely result in the failure of your second location—and may drag down your first one as well.

Don't think too small or too big as you open your center.

(See Chapter 6 for more on staff issues, as well as Key #2 in Chapter 9).

#2 New Business Mistake To Avoid—Losing Your Focus

Too many new business owners get so caught up in the excitement of opening their own business that they overwork themselves. They end up burned out soon after launch, especially if the grand opening wasn't as grand as they'd been hoping.

They get discouraged and frightened that this thing isn't going to work after all, and they make rash decisions. When they don't see the immediate rewards they were hoping for, they may even decide their center is a failure and drop the business venture altogether.

Don't make this mistake. No matter what happens in your first days, remember that opening a new business is a long-term project. You need to stay the course. You need to remain focused.

Yes, you are going to work long hours. That goes with the

territory. Just take care of yourself along the way. Be sure to take breaks and not exhaust yourself. Fatigue can bring on depression, panic, and a complete loss of perspective.

The good news for you is that, in LearningRx, you've selected a business and service that stirs your passions. Keep remembering why you got into this franchise in the first place and you will be able to maintain your focus.

Don't be Superman or Superwoman. Be a super delegator.

(See Chapter 1 for more on this).

#3 New Business Mistake To Avoid—Taking on Too Much by Yourself

No one can do everything himself. Not even you. If you try, you may end up losing your energy and perspective, as I just discussed.

It is always a good idea to seek the help of others. This can be through employees or professional services. When you have other people doing the details, you can focus your energy on the bigger goals and strategies that concern your center.

As a LearningRx franchisee, you can take advantage of the corporate system we have in place. Do so! Use the backbone marketing program, work with your account executive to create action plans, and communicate with other franchisees to exchange ideas and receive support.

Don't be Superman or Superwoman. Be a super delegator.

(See Chapters 7 and 8 for more on this, and Key #4 in Chapter 9).

#4 New Business Mistake To Avoid—Not Tracking Advertising Properly

When you pay to advertise your business it's important to know if your money is being spent effectively or not. What's the point of spending thousands of dollars for a billboard that never generates new customers?

Whenever you purchase advertising, always make sure you can track the return on investment (ROI) so you can allocate more money for those that provide a higher return.

Advertising is a tricky thing. It's very easy for a business to throw away a lot of money on advertising that is virtually worthless. Do experiments. Watch for surges that might be connected to your advertising. Ask people how they heard about you and train your staff to do the same. And be specific: If you're running an ad on two radio stations and the potential customer says "I heard it on the radio," ask which one. And don't be afraid to pull the plug on advertising channels that aren't producing for you.

(For more on this, see Key #5 in Chapter 10).

#5 New Business Mistake To Avoid—Not Getting Involved in the Community

It may come as a surprise to you, but business owners do better when they take a break from their businesses to get involved in the community.

Attending local events and becoming an active member of the community are great ways to get free attention for your business. Networking is an important part of building up good business relationships that can lead directly to customer opportunities.

It's all about who you know.

(See Chapter 9, Key #7 for more on this).

#6 New Business Mistake To Avoid—Not Having Cash Flow

Cash flow is the lifeblood of all businesses. If you run out of cash your business will fail. You must manage your cash with the care and attention it deserves, knowing exactly what your cash balance is. Don't manage from your bank balance. You reconcile your bank balance—you don't manage from it. You need enough cash so you are free to do what you do best: taking care of clients and making more money.

(I covered this in detail in Chapter 10).

#7 New Business Mistake To Avoid—Working in the Business but Not on the Business

If you define your job as being the person who prepares your business for growth, you are working *on* your business. That's as it should be. But if you are consumed with doing every important thing yourself, you are working *in* your business—not on it.

The ultimate goal of working *on* your business should be to have it function as well as possible without you. Getting your business to this point is not going to happen overnight. It takes a conscious, sustained effort and time. If you want to make it happen, you have to make it happen! Work *on* your business not just *in* it.

(Chapters 5 and 6 explain this more).

Conclusion

Use this chapter's list as a quick summary for success in your franchise. All of these points are covered in detail elsewhere in the book but sometimes it's nice to have an at-a-glance guide to help you keep your finger on the pulse of your business.

I want you to succeed. I want your LearningRx center to become one of our premier locations. And I want you to succeed personally as a franchisee. This whole book has been written to help you achieve your goals. I hope this quick summary will add to your sense of being fully equipped to help you avoid the mines and take your franchise to the place you want it to go.

If you have followed, or will diligently follow, the values, strategies, and profit principles discussed in this and previous chapters, then there is a very high probability that more revenue will come your way than you can currently spend. That's not to say you can't learn to spend it. But is it the right option for you? In the next chapter I'll share with you my perspective of wealth and how to handle excess revenues. You may choose not to share my views, because they are not the norm, but considering these thoughts might greatly enrich your life.

CHAPTER 14

Stewardship & Giving

WEALTH IS LIKE a Coke® bottle.

The Gods Must Be Crazy is a low-budget comedy film about what happens when a pilot passing over the plains of Africa drops his Coca-Cola® bottle out of the plane. The glass bottle lands in the village in the Kalahari Desert and is picked up by Xi, a Sho native.

Xi and his fellow villagers believe a god has cast the strange object out of the heavens. At first, they suppose the thing to be an object for their benefit. They discover that the clear but oddly strong item is excellent for smashing gourds and grinding grain and handling a variety of tasks about the village. Suddenly, everyone wants the thing. And then everyone needs the thing. It isn't long before one of them uses it to strike someone in anger.

Then Xi decides that the gods must've dropped the item by mistake. To him, the object is obviously evil and his village needs to be rid of it before it destroys them. So he sets out on an epic quest to take the thing to the edge of the world and give it back to the gods.

Wealth Is Like That

A sudden windfall of money is like that glass bottle falling from the sky. It looks appealing at first. It seems like it will be the answer to all your problems. But then it shows its power to corrupt and enslave and turn people against one another.

Wealth's most natural ability is the ability to destroy contentment.

When before, the old clunker car had been all right, now it's terrible and in need of replacement. When the small home in the suburbs had been enough before, now it's an embarrassment and must be swapped out for something befitting your new status. When once you'd had enough to be comfortable, now there always seems to be one more thing you need.

Oh, for the day when you were content with food to eat and a roof over your head!

Xi figured out the way to handle wealth. He held it reluctantly, as if it were radioactive, because he knew how dangerous it could be.

I'm not saying that wealth is inherently evil. When you compare the United States to all other nations, you see that even the poorest American has more than the average person globally.

I'm not advocating a complete downsizing to a cardboard box and a shopping cart. What I'm saying is that we tend to have the wrong notion about wealth. It can be a blessing or it can bring serious harm to our businesses, our families, and us.

The Right Understanding of Wealth

Here's a story from my daughter Kim:

> *Growing up in a house with five kids and a frugal dad meant there was a lot of sharing. We would share meals, gifts, and toys. In seventh grade I started working at my dad's office and was required to buy my own stuff. That's when sharing didn't seem fair. If I bought a bag of chips with my own money I had to share it with my brothers and sisters, even though sometimes I didn't feel like it. My sisters liked my cool clothes and would sneak up into my room and take what they wanted.*
>
> *I'd go down and complain to my dad, but his answer was always the same: "Everything belongs to God, Kim. We are only caretakers of His things. What would He want you to do?"*
>
> *"But if I'm the caretaker shouldn't I get to determine if I share or not?"*
>
> *"Yes, you should. So…what would God want you do to?"*
>
> *For years this was confusing to me, but I finally got it. God gives and takes away, and we need to be good stewards of whatever He gives. My dad modeled this for me. And now, if you were to ask my kids who something belongs to, they'd tell you it belongs to God.*

I believe we are essentially asset managers.

An asset manager is someone who takes responsibility over a client's stocks, bonds, real estate, etc., and manages them to meet the client's goals. An asset manager basically takes the client's wealth and works with it to try to bring about more wealth or to otherwise manage it according to the client's wishes.

It's the modern term for a *steward*. A steward was a servant who took care of someone else's land, home, flocks, money, and belongings in order to achieve the master's purposes. Whenever the master went away, the steward was in charge of everything, handling it in the way the master would want.

> *It's not how much wealth you have; it's how you deal with the resources you've been given.*

We should be stewards. We've been given various forms of wealth: abilities, attributes, intelligence, talents, time, relationships, and financial resources. I believe none of it is ours. It all belongs to the Master. And though we're allowed to make use of it here, we're doing so at the behest of someone else, someone who will want to know what we've done with what He put us in charge of while we were here.

Wealth, like any other resource we've been asked to manage, isn't evil—it's neutral. But it *is* dangerous, as Xi discovered with the Coke® bottle. It does have the power to corrupt and divide and to cancel out the blissful contentment we'd enjoyed before it came.

You play the hand you're dealt. Riches constitute one of the hands you've been dealt in this life. Maybe it's a royal flush or maybe it's only a pair of twos. Either way, what matters isn't how much wealth you have; what matters is how you deal with the resources you've been given.

You are responsible for how you react to the opportunities set before you. The response is up to you—and it reveals your character.

Some people are dealt a weak hand when it comes to finances. So what? Those people still have to respond well to the hand they've been dealt. Others are dealt a stronger hand, financially speaking. Again, so what? It's something they were given, not something they did themselves. I like football coach Barry Switzer's comment: "Some people are born on third base and go through life thinking they hit a triple."

Some folks are dealt a strong hand in terms of health and relationships but a weak hand in talents and money. Others are flush with time but have very little in terms of health. Each resource is a hand you're dealt. You'll be strong in some suits and weak in others. That's the way the cards are dealt. So what?

Everyone does not have the same hand. But everyone is faced with the same mandate: deal rightly with what you've been given. We are to be like the steward whose master is going away on a trip and leaving him in charge. The master hands him some resources and says, "Do business with all this until I return."

How are you doing as an asset manager? You don't have all the master's wealth, certainly, but you have some of it. How are you investing it? You don't have every talent or skill under the sun, but you have some. How are you investing them? What about the time that is yours to spend? What about the relationships in your care? How are you pursuing the Master's goals with the portion of His estate He's left you in charge of?

In the parable referenced above, the master returns from his trip and calls his stewards to account. Those who invested his assets wisely are rewarded with increased responsibility and honor in the master's estate. Those who invested poorly or not at all are punished.

The little we're charged with managing is our testing for how much we'll be given in the future. "To everyone who has, more shall be given, but from the one who does not have, even what he does have shall be taken away."

How you manage your resources matters.

The Purpose of Possessions

I believe there are three purposes for possessions. The first is the provision of basic needs. The second is the celebration of life. And the third is service.

Basic Needs

A wise man said, "If we have food and clothing, we will be content with that." He was expressing an understanding of possessions. He knew that we need a few things to sustain life, but that's about all we truly need.

We certainly want more than that. Our lives would be more comfortable if we also had a decent place to live, a means of transportation, heating and cooling, running water, and the like. But if you were to boil it all down to the basic requirements, we don't need much.

Most people think they have too little, but I disagree. I believe I have been given everything I need for what I need to do. If I needed more, more would be given to me. So how am I going to use what I've received?

That perspective takes a lot of the pressure off, I think. We have—right now—exactly the amount of resources we need. Now we can quit worrying about the more or less of it and concentrate on applying what we have been given in support of our purpose.

So long as our basic needs are met, we have enough. But sometimes we're given possessions beyond those basics. This is good and bad. It's good because we can enjoy it. It's bad if this elevated level of belongings becomes what we consider our minimum requirements.

When I was 12, my dad took me on a fishing trip in the boundary waters of northern Minnesota. After four days of catching nothing and being hungry I ate something I detested—Lipton® split-pea soup. It was fantastic, the best soup I'd ever had. A week later at home, after requesting it, I couldn't keep it down. It is so easy to become spoiled with all the abundance around us.

We can rejoice in our added possessions. But with added resources comes added responsibilities. "From everyone who has been given much, much will be required; and to whom they entrusted much, of him they will ask all the more."

To the degree that you have been given abundance above the basic needs, to that same degree you'll be asked to be a faithful steward.

Be careful what you wish for.

The Celebration of Life

The first purpose of possessions is to provide for our basic needs. The second is to allow us to celebrate life.

Did you catch that? You have been supplied with things so you can enjoy them. Enjoy what has been provided for you.

Is it possible to go across the line from enjoyment into indulgence? Sure. But where that line is, is something you have to decide. It will vary from person to person and probably from time to time even with the same person.

We must beware of setting ourselves up as judge when other people look as if they have moved into overindulgence. That's a matter with that person—not us. I don't know about you, but I have enough trouble trying to find that line for myself without trying to establish it for anyone else.

Years ago, one family member responded to an opportunity that other family members chose not to. That choice eventually turned a very small investment into a $50 million windfall. Fortunately, in our family the judging and resentment about this has not been visible, but we must remain on guard because our heart tends to judge others who are more fortunate.

Service

The third purpose for possessions is service. We have been given resources so we can use them to meet the needs of others.

You have a chainsaw and your elderly neighbor needs wood cut for the winter? Do the math. You have an extra car and someone on your block needs a vehicle to get back and forth to work? You have a large house and a family in your city has lost their home to fire? You love children and the Big Brothers and Sisters in your area needs volunteers? You have a rare blood type?

I'm not saying you have to give to every need that comes along. That's a good way to feel guilty all the time. Your purpose will guide you here (see Chapter 1). What I'm saying is that you're a *steward*; an asset manager. And when a need is brought to your attention, sometimes that's a clue for you to cut a check, literally or figuratively, from the assets you're managing to help alleviate the anxiety or suffering around you.

Possessions and other resources are good things. They're part of the estate that's been left in your care. You already have exactly enough of them or something will happen to change how much you have.

Wealth

You've heard people misquote this phrase, I'm sure. They say, "Money is the root of all evil."

Too bad they got it wrong. Money isn't the root of all evil, any more than guns murder people. Money is neutral, like the poppy seed, which can be used to create either delightful muffins or heroin. It's not money that is the root of all evil, it's the love of it. Here's the correct phrase: "The love of money is a root of all sorts of evil."

For years I was very confused on this point. I felt that making too much money was bad, a sin of some sort. I would start a business, get it producing a nice profit, and then either give it away or sabotage it. It wasn't until after listening to Tony Robbins, a motivation guru, define money as something other than dollars that I could feel good about earning money.

Today I define income as *a measure of the help I'm able to give others*. Suddenly, it's a good thing to earn lots of money. Now I'm in a position to help others.

However, there is a major difference between earning money and accumulating money. For me, accumulating beyond what I need to meet my basic needs and a reasonable celebration of life is just hoarding. But using any additional earning to serve others creates a double good: the good I create in earning by serving and the good created by giving to others my earnings that are beyond my needs.

But this runs counter to our culture, doesn't it? In our world you're not somebody unless you have a lot of loot. If you don't drive an expensive car, wear high-priced jewelry, dress in designer clothes, or live in a big house, you're a nobody.

And we buy into that idea (literally), as our many debts testify. Credit cards fuel an artificial feeling of wealth and give the illusion of riches. We chase after it, and sometimes wander away and find ourselves pierced with many griefs. Credit card bills being one of them.

Here are a few other dangers of wealth:

- Wealth creates a false sense of independence and security—who needs someone else when you can buy yourself out of any problem?

- Wealth creates fuzzy thinking about our importance— maybe I really am superior to the 'little people'

- Wealth tempts us with greed and a desire for more and more

Keep in mind that wealth is like that bottle that fell on Xi's head in the desert. It seems desirable but it can prove to be destructive. Riches are safe only when handled carefully—as if you're dealing with radioactive waste. Wealth, like radiation, can be a great benefit if used correctly. But it can easily burn you too.

And yet sometimes we are granted riches. Viewed correctly, wealth can be a great blessing.

If you find yourself suddenly wealthier (or suddenly poorer), beware. Any time we experience a shift from one standard to another it will cause stress in our lives. Sudden financial loss can result in compensation, as we override the shift by going into debt. But sudden financial gain can be just as damaging, as a glance at the personal lives of many Lotto winners or college-athletes-turned-pro will illustrate.

Nevertheless, if you develop a wholesome mindset toward whatever you have—wealth, poverty, or something in between—you can find peace in the midst of it. You need to cultivate thankfulness, stewardship, and contentment.

Wealth handled in this way can be a blessing to you and those around you. Here are two benefits of wealth:

- Wealth can help you celebrate life

- Wealth can provide you with the opportunity to invest in higher purposes

Years ago, I put certain business structures in place that would help us guard against indulgence. It was a few years before starting LearningRx and I was beginning to grasp the financial potential of what we were developing. I wanted to hold to the values I'd taught my family—and to steer clear of my past desires for accumulating wealth. I'll share these with you here.

However, I'm not suggesting that you need to do the same. I'm revealing them here as an illustration of what an unbelievable blessing our family has received as a result of putting structures in place that support our values.

I decided to give the legal ownership of 95 percent of my intellectual property to my family (in a family limited partnership), with the condition that 50 percent of net earnings from that property be given to charitable causes. This guaranteed that no one else could go crazy with accumulation, as half the earnings had to go to charitable giving.

This one decision has unified our family around purposes larger than ourselves. Our whole endeavor is focused on giving instead of getting. I can't begin to share with you the tremendous sense of caring, sharing love, and unity that results from our family meetings when we determine why, when, where, and which charitable groups we want to support. Involving my 11 grandchildren in this activity is one of my greatest pleasures. It will leave them a legacy of stewardship and caring beyond what I could ever teach them through word or print.

This structure has one other benefit for us: It helps us make decisions not based on personal gain.

I have heard some wealthy people imply that God is pleased by their shrewd investments, that He is better glorified when His children are wealthy than when they are poor. I disagree. We don't please God on the basis of our canny investments but on whether or not we use *whatever we've been given* for good.

I believe that it's better to be a good steward of what you've been given than to become rich.

Contentment

This is a word I've used a few times already in this chapter. You know what contentment means. You've probably experienced it in your life. And if you're like most people, you've experienced the lack of it too.

Contentment might be defined as a peaceful satisfaction with one's situation in life. It is ease of mind, a happy state in which you do not feel you are lacking anything you need.

...contentment is what happens when you decide that everything you have is all you need.

How often do you feel this way? Is it your normal state of mind or have you experienced it only fleetingly, such as when you've won the championship or bought the house of your dreams?

I'm going to say something right now that may sound crazy. You ready? Contentment is a choice.

I told you it would sound wild. Most people think contentment is what happens when you get everything you want, but who ever gets that? Contentment isn't what happens when you get everything you want; *contentment is what happens when you decide that everything you already have is all you need*—even if you have nothing but food and clothing. It's when you realize, "Hey, I've got enough right now. I've got *more* than enough. I don't need anything else. I might even be able to give some of this stuff away to someone else."

Are you there? Do you look at your basic needs and realize that not only are they met, but also that you have a lot of other things that many people don't have? Sure, you could get a bigger this or a newer that, but chasing after those things is futile.

Stop the chase, why don't you? Redraw the circle that says, "I'll be happy when X comes into my circle." Cast the circle again so that it includes your basic needs only. When you do that, you'll see that you already have the thing you've been knocking yourself out to get.

Contentment is being OK with whatever comes your way. Whether it's wealth or poverty or something in the middle. Whether it's health or sickness, safety or peril, peace or crisis—in it, you'll be able to rest in a peace unlike any the world gives. That doesn't mean you have to jump for joy when tragedy comes or when things don't work out as you'd hoped. But it means your contentment, your sense that all is right with the world, is not touched, come what may.

I love the story of how the hymn "It Is Well with My Soul" was written. Horatio Spafford was an American lawyer-turned-hymnist in the late nineteenth century. He suffered many appalling tragedies in his life. His only son died from illness in 1871. That same year the Great Chicago Fire ruined him financially. And in an accident at sea two years later, all four of his daughters were drowned.

Soon after this last loss, while in a ship passing near the spot where his daughters had been killed, he was inspired to write the words to an incredible song, which begins like this:

When peace like a river attendeth my way,
When sorrows like sea billows roll;
Whatever my lot, Thou hast taught me to say,
It is well, it is well, with my soul.

How about you? Is it well with your soul, even though sorrows are rolling like the billows of the sea that took your beloved?

Contentment like this is a choice. It is something you can have by understanding simple ideas like:

- My Maker is in control and He is good—and what comes into my life is for my benefit, though I may not be able to see it now.

- Trials and hardships come to develop and display my character.

If you lack contentment, it may be because you do not yet believe these things. When you do, contentment will come.

If you lack contentment you'll be motivated by all the wrong things. You'll be trying to go out and find something to fill this awful, yawning emptiness you feel.

I have found that discontented people fall into two categories— both unpleasant. On the one hand you have those whose discontentment propels them to try to change their situation to match what they think contentment looks like. They're dissatisfied with who they are, what they are, and what they have, so they're out agitating for improvement. The truth is that no amount of stuff, no matter how good or how much, will ever satisfy.

On the other hand, you have those whose discontentment causes them to retreat from life. They feel vulnerable and lacking and probably have been deeply hurt. And so they retract into a defensive position in which they feel they can insulate themselves from further hurt. They, unlike the other group, are not motivated to do anything. They're passive, complacent. They have little ambition or motivation in life. On the surface they may appear satisfied because they don't seem to be striving for "more," but in reality they're operating out of a sense of hopeless emptiness they believe can never be filled.

Whether you have wealth or poverty, contentment is the greater possession. Contentment allows peace, like a river, to attend your soul. Contentment sails you across rolling waters in a deep sense of ease.

Giving and Receiving

Earlier I talked about three purposes for wealth: the supply of basic needs, the enjoyment of life, and the service of others. Here are two more comments.

The ultimate privilege of having an abundance of any resource, financial or otherwise, is the ability to join in a greater purpose. We do that through giving. Let me say it this way: when you give, *you are being like God*, who gives to all generously and without reproach.

The second comment is about the other side of giving: receiving. Giving and receiving have been compared to breathing. You can't exhale unless you also inhale, after all.

I used to have a hard time accepting compliments or allowing people to pay for my meal or the like. Yet I expected others to accept my gifts. Once, after arguing over who was going to pick up the tab for lunch, a friend said, "Ken, this time let me pick this up so I can get the joy of giving to you. Don't rob me of that blessing." That put a whole different light on it. I suddenly realized there was a need for me to become a gracious receiver.

Since that lunch I've made it a point to say, "Thank you" when given a compliment or meal.

Recently, I received a very large gift that really shook me. I didn't want to accept it. I felt it was too much.

My wife had been wanting a custom log cabin in the mountains. She even had *Log Home Living* magazine coming to our home each month. My kids had been wanting a place where all the grandchildren could get together away from Colorado Springs— like the northern Wisconsin cottage my parents had when my kids were growing up.

To end this pressure, I agreed to take a day to look at some cabins. My goal was twofold: I wanted to convince them that this wasn't needed and that we wouldn't be able to find anything that met my criteria. My criteria were that it would:

- be within two hours of Colorado Springs
- have large custom logs
- have two levels (so that the grandchildren could play in an area separate from the adults)
- have a stone fireplace
- have ample sleeping room for the whole family (21 members at the time)
- be near skiing and restaurants
- cost at least $100K under the market value
- be secluded but with easy access to major roads
- and (the really big criteria) that it would be on water, which is almost impossible to find in Colorado

A lot of that list resulted from me visualizing a cabin I'd seen numerous times on trips to Breckenridge. With a list like that I knew I was safe. But if my family wanted me to go driving around in the mountains of Colorado for a day, I figured I could "take one for the team." So a big group of us went on our search.

The third log home we were shown that Saturday was the exact cabin I had used to create my list.

As I entered, I realized that it met all my criteria. I'd laid out a fleece as great as Gideon's, and here it all was—including the price. I broke down and bawled so badly that I had to excuse myself to a bedroom.

How could I accept this? It was too much, too extravagant. I believe we are to use the money we're given to celebrate life, as I've said, but this seemed beyond what I would consider an acceptable celebration of life. I didn't need or even want something this nice. I didn't deserve it. *God, why would You give this to us?*

At that moment, one of the kids opened the door to the bedroom and urged me to come see something. It was a picture on the wall that contained subject material so personal to our family that I knew this was beyond chance. My bawling intensified. It confirmed to me that God wanted to bless me far beyond what I could ever conceive. At that moment I wasn't the giver; I was the receiver. And I knew that I needed to thankfully accept His unmerited gift.

Conclusion

It is likely that you have wealth to some degree. Probably you would not be a LearningRx franchisee if you had no financial resources at all. Your basic needs have been met and you are in a position to bless others with the excess.

Your LearningRx franchise is a tangible channel through which you can extend the giving. You are bringing hope and help and improvement that will change lives and bestow glad futures.

You also have other resources that have been given over to you as asset manager. How are you investing them?

Don't weary yourself in the useless pursuit of wealth. Instead, be content with what you have. Enjoy the things you've been given and always be on the lookout for how you can apply those resources toward those who need your love.

Seek contentment and the wisdom about how to invest whatever it is you have been given to steward. Handled carefully and with the right attitude, the Coke® bottle of wealth can bring great blessing to your village.

Purpose & Success Revisited

AS YOU'VE READ through this book you've no doubt noticed references to God and the Bible. As I was editing the manuscript I actually removed many additional such references, as I wanted this book to be a business book rather than a religious book.

In graduate school, I learned that professionals don't mix religion into their professional practice. For years I accepted that concept. I meticulously segregated my spiritual life from my secular life. But I don't believe that anymore. I've learned that living on Sunday in a way that is different from how you live the rest of the week may help you get by easier, but it's hypocritical.

This book has been written to help you succeed. If you succeed in business, I'll be pleased. And if the book helps you in life, I'll be even happier. But if it helps you find your purpose—which, I believe, can be found only in your Creator—I'll be ecstatic.

In the last three years before I wrote this book our family had three near-death experiences. Three. In one case, a near-drowning, in another, a lung infection, and in the other, a drug overdose. In all cases they were truly almost fatal. Either the breathing, the heart, or the brain—or some combination—had stopped.

Do you know what it's like to see your 3-year-old vivacious grandson floating face up, under the water, motionless? I can tell you from experience. Do you know what it's like to hear that your beautiful, bright, and talented 24-year-old niece is unable to breathe? I do. Do you know what it's like to watch a very caring family member lying brain dead at the hospital as doctors prepare to pull the plug? I know what that's like. Because I lived it.

Praise God—all three are alive today.

It's easy for these types of circumstances to cause us to ask *why*. Why did these three precious people have to come so close to death? Maybe the better question is why were they brought back? They were at death's door but were turned back for more life. Why? What purpose does God have in mind?

That's a great question. What purpose does God have in mind? Why am I still here? Is there something left for me to do?

I hope you don't have to face a near-death experience to ask that question about yourself. I believe that the glory of any created thing is to fulfill its created purpose. If that's true, what is your purpose and what are you doing about fulfilling it?

Principles of Success

- Purpose instills your life with a sense of meaning, passion, and purpose

- Truthfulness establishes trust with others

- Don't waste your suffering: Let it be an opportunity for growth

- When things go well, look through the window; when things go badly, look in the mirror

- Nurturing negative thinking is like taking poison and waiting for others to die

- Decisiveness is not so much the ability to think quickly as the ability to compare the opportunity with your purpose

- Always seek refinements to enhance what you're doing

- The unfocused use of your time is a sure path to mediocrity in business

- If one person casts a vision and many people catch it, everything can be changed

- Concentrate first on the biggest priorities and the lesser priorities will fall into place

- Break goals down into bite-sized tasks

- Your influence is determined by the degree you place other people's interests above your own

- With every pair of hands you hire, you get a free brain

- When you are a server to your customers and staff, they will follow you

- Marketing is not an expense; it is an investment and drives your revenue

- Your value is determined by how much more you give than take

- Treat your customers not only as you would want to be treated, but as you want your staff to treat customers

- Budget a profit

- It's not how much wealth you have; it's how you deal with the resources you've been given

- Your earnings are determined by how many people you serve and how well you serve them

- Contentment is what happens when you decide that everything you already have is all you need

- You cannot fully give until you can also graciously receive

- The glory of any created thing is to fulfill its created purpose